THE MAKING OF

Jane Austen's EMMA

SUE BIRTWISTLE & SUSIE CONKLIN

D1421991

PENGUIN BOOKS

For the two
Richards
(Eyre and Taylor)

Penguin Books
Published by the Penguin Group
Penguin Books Ltd, 27 Wrights Lane, London w8 5tz, England
Penguin Books USA Inc. 375 Hudson Street, New York, New York 10014, USA
Penguin Books Australia Ltd, Ringwood, Victoria, Australia
Penguin Books Canada Ltd, 10 Alcorn Avenue, Toronto, Ontario, Canada m4v 3b2
Penguin Books (NZ) Ltd, 182–190 Wairau Road Auckland 10, New Zealand

Penguin Books Ltd, Registered Offices: Harmondsworth, Middlesex, England

First published 1996
1 3 5 7 9 10 8 6 7 2

Made and printed in Great Britain by
Butler and Tanner Ltd, Frome
Colour reproduction by Radstock Reproductions, Midsomer Norton

Contents

Introduction

WHEN we finished our last book, *The Making of Pride and Prejudice*, the television programme itself was still several months away from being screened and we couldn't have guessed at the overwhelming reaction it would produce. Nor, because of this, how many people would buy the book. All this, of course, was very gratifying, but we were taken aback by how carefully both the programme and the book were scrutinized and how many letters were written as a result. Between the cast, writer, director, the BBC and ourselves, we received – quite literally – thousands. And very fortunate we were in our correspondents.

Of course, there were several of the 'why, oh why?' variety that we'd anticipated, like the 'horticulturalist' who'd spotted, in the background of a shot, roses that hadn't been introduced into England until 1830, or the military man who sent ten closely-typed pages, upbraiding us about the flashes on the soldiers' uniforms, or the viewer whose enjoyment had been ruined by catching a glimpse of limestone as the coach wheels passed, thus showing it couldn't have been Hertfordshire.

But, on the whole, the letters brimmed over with delight and far more praise than anyone has a right to expect in one lifetime. Most of this, quite rightly, was directed at the cast. It was interesting that not only did the letters come from all ages (the youngest from two seven-year-olds who had fallen for Mr Darcy, the oldest, a 92-year-old woman, who was also rather keen on him, though in a rather more forthright way: 'P.S. Mr Darcy can share my shower any day he likes!') but also from men as well as women. Some were very touching, some very funny, most were very kind. Many made suggestions for future projects and one woman even wrote her own new ending to *Pride and Prejudice* which was so racy that even Andrew Davies blushed. Hundreds of students sent in detailed questionnaires for help with their Austen essays but, although we answered all the letters, we had to draw the line at this equivalent of writing several examination papers.

Whilst all this was happening, we were already at work on *Emma*. This time, Andrew Davies had proposed the project. Not that it was difficult to persuade us; we'd had such fun making *Pride and Prejudice* that to be allowed to make another Jane Austen was a delight. But, before anyone asks, we don't intend to romp through the rest of her novels.

As we write this, *Emma* is still being edited and will be shown in November. In this book, we've incorporated some of the suggestions we received after the last one. We have included the screenplay or, at least, the screenplay as it was filmed. Keen-eyed people will notice that not all of it is in the finished film (though we hope no one will sit with it on their lap as they watch!) It's not a how-to-film book this time, following everyone's jobs; rather it concentrates on certain aspects of making *Emma*. You won't find anything about the post-production work – the music, editing or sound dubbing – as this is all still happening as the book goes to the printers.

We have one request: if you haven't yet read Jane Austen's book or seen our film, then please don't read beyond here until you have. Part of the novel is a hidden detective story and, inevitably, we will refer to incidents or parts of the plot that will give away these secrets and spoil your first enjoyment of the piece.

Sue Birtwistle (Producer) and Susie Conklin (Script Editor)
September 1996

CHAPTER I

The script

EMMA is one of Jane Austen's great novels. Many would argue it is her finest, but it posed many difficulties in adapting it for television. The main character is a spoilt and snobbish young woman whose actions often appal us, the romantic hero must remain disguised for at least half of the story, and the plot appears to revolve around Emma's often disastrous attempts at match-making. Meanwhile, a complex detective story lies underneath which unfolds so subtly that most readers don't pick it up on the first reading of the book.

Despite these challenges, the novel offers a brilliant variety of characters and a rich seam of humour and irony, which adapter Andrew Davies believes lends itself wonderfully well to a dramatic treatment. Director Diarmuid Lawrence agrees: 'It's richly ironic and bitterly funny and can amuse you at the same time as showing how foolish people can be. It also has a strong romantic vein. Although all Austen's earlier novels show consumate skill in any one of those areas, I still think that *Emma* is the one that is the richest.'

The length of the adaptation was a key factor in determining how the story should be told. Although the novel is longer than *Pride and Prejudice* (which was screened as a six-part serial) Andrew Davies soon determined that it would work much better at a shorter length. 'Nick Elliott at the ITV Network Centre said he was keen on doing it as a two-hour film if that was possible, and it turned out to be a very good idea. Though *Emma* is a long and complex novel, there's not a tremendous lot of plot to it. The screenplay is pared pretty close to the narrative bone, but it can work. In the book the ending seems to go on for ever, whereas in the drama you don't want this very, very lengthy tying up of loose ends, explanations and afterthoughts. For example, Frank Churchill writes this great enormous letter explain-

By the end of filming, Kate's script is well-thumbed and coffee stained.

OPPOSITE: *Mrs Weston and Emma in the Hartfield garden.*

*Andrew Davies, Sue Birtwistle
and Diarmuid Lawrence watch
the filming.*

*Emma decides that Harriet's 'soft
blue eyes and natural graces should
not be wasted on the inferior society
of Highbury' (Jane Austen).*

ing himself, but unlike Darcy's letter in *Pride and Prejudice*, it is not instrumental in furthering the plot.'

Diarmuid thought the two-hour length was also the most appropriate for dealing with a character like Emma's. 'One of the reasons why the dynamic of *Emma* works better for me as a single film is that it helps to reinforce the swings of feelings you have towards Emma – from wanting to smack her at one end to falling in love with her at the other. During the course of the film she goes from being adorably mischievous, to being dangerous and venomous to Harriet, to being someone we are entirely captivated by at the end. I think it's easier to do that in one film than across several episodes.'

In spite of these advantages, this compression meant that many difficult decisions had to be made about which events from the book should be left in and which should be taken out. Emma's various attempts at match-making Mr Elton with Harriet, for example, were trimmed down in order to give enough time to develop Frank Churchill's complex story in the second half of the film. Although many of these scenes between Emma and Mr Elton are delightful, such as the offering of the courtship riddle, they did hold up the narrative. Another example is the introduction of Jane Fairfax. News of Jane comes early in the book, even before her arrival in Highbury. But Andrew felt it was better to wait until the audience had seen her before it heard stories of her predicament. However, by far the most important decision involved the handling of the events at the end of the book. Andrew reworked all these into one big new scene – a harvest supper. *(See Chapter Five.)*

A HEROINE 'WHOM NO ONE BUT MYSELF WILL MUCH LIKE' *(Jane Austen)*

Emma is not a typical Austen heroine. 'Jane Austen's usual heroine is somebody who life or society has placed at a disadvantage – like the girls in *Pride and Prejudice* or *Sense and Sensibility*,' says Andrew. 'But that's not the case with Emma. She's the stuck-up girl who has everything.' Certainly she possesses every advantage in life – she is rich, beautiful, doted upon by her father and governess, and is top of the social hierarchy in Highbury. Unlike most of Austen's other heroines, Emma doesn't need to marry for financial security which, as she points out to Harriet one day, means she can see no reason for marrying at all. But these aren't the only qualities which set her apart. More disturbingly, particularly for a modern audience, she's a social snob who wants everything done on her own terms, and she interferes (often with disastrous results) in other people's lives. Without softening Jane Austen's intentions for television, there was a need to dramatize her in such a way as to prevent the audience from switching off.

'The first time I read the novel I thought, in a sort of superior way, "Oh, but I like Emma",' says Andrew. 'But in the next four readings I thought, "Jane, you're right, I don't like this girl much at all." Then I had this idea that perhaps Jane Austen said she was a heroine that "no one would like but myself" because Emma is a kind of artist. She has an artistic sensibility, which is much like that of a novelist. In a way she doesn't want to be involved in life, she just wants to run it; she wants to be God and move the pieces around the board; she wants to plan the plot and create the characters. She wants to change Harriet from an innocent young girl into a fascinating charmer.

'I think in a practical way, this was my starting point with Emma. This idea of Emma having an artistic sensibility and wanting to manipulate life was something I treated as a playful thing, showing that the exuberant imagination she has makes her want to embellish every story she hears. She imagines things and then exaggerates them. I thought it would be good to see Emma's fantasies on screen. So, when she hears a brief account of the story of Mr Dixon saving Jane Fairfax from falling overboard in a squall at Weymouth, we see Emma imagining a very romantic overblown thing where Mr Dixon snatches Jane from the raging sea and clutches her to his bosom.'

This device of dramatizing Emma's fantasies allows us to enjoy her wild imagination. 'It makes her much more likeable, because we all day-dream,' says Andrew. 'Though the funny thing is that we tend to day-dream about ourselves, picturing romantic things that might happen to us, whereas Emma fantasises about other people. She doesn't want to be in love herself. She's a novelist manquée.'

Another important means of understanding Emma, is seeing her in the context of the world in which she lives. The script begins with the wedding of her much-loved governess, Miss Taylor. We see that Emma is genuinely happy for her friend, though Mr Woodhouse's response is simply selfish; for him it can only be a sad business. The sharp cut, from seeing Emma waving off the newly-weds in their carriage to her sitting at dinner alone with her father, tells the larger story. The table is far too big for two people, and we quickly perceive that Mr Woodhouse is no companion for Emma. Though he is often unintentionally amusing, Mr Woodhouse is possibly the most trying father anyone could imagine. He is a hypochondriac obsessed with his own maladies, who sees marriage, travel, and people outside his tiny social circle as evils to be avoided. He shows a complete lack of sensitivity or understanding to the needs of his bright 21-year-old daughter. Given how little companionship she gets from him, Emma's extraordinary kindness and attention towards her father is one mark of her true generosity of spirit.

'In the end I feel a bit sorry for Emma,' says Andrew. 'She finishes up married to one of the three blokes she's ever known; the fur-

Emma's vivid imagination exaggerates the boating incident off Weymouth.

Mr Woodhouse to Emma: 'Pray do not make any more matches, they are silly things, and break up one's family circle grievously' (Jane Austen).

Emma finds Jane 'disgustingly reserved' (Jane Austen).

Jane's only way of expressing her passionate feelings is through her music.

thest she's ever been from home is Box Hill; and everything goes wrong when she steps out of her backyard. She hasn't had a chance to see much of life. In a way I think that Jane Austen was trying to create something fascinating, intricate and exciting out of the materials of a very dull life.'

JANE FAIRFAX AND FRANK CHURCHILL

In any other Austen novel, Jane Fairfax would be the story's protagonist. Though beautiful, intelligent and talented, her lack of family or personal fortune means she is destined to be a governess. Whilst her situation arouses the sympathies of most of the Highbury circle, Emma appears unmoved. She is somewhat intimidated by Jane's beauty and musical talents, but it is Jane's reserved nature that really annoys Emma. Jane has already met Frank Churchill, something Emma and the whole of Highbury have been longing to do. When Emma, in an effort to make friends with her, asks Jane what she thought of him, the sort of questions she asks are natural: is he handsome? Is he agreeable? What did you think of him? Jane's refusal to give a satisfactory reply to any of her questions only confirm Emma's views on Jane. 'There was no getting at her real opinion. Wrapt up in a cloak of politeness, she seemed determined to hazard nothing. She was disgustingly, was suspiciously reserved. Emma could not forgive her.' It is very easy for the audience to take Emma's side here, but as Andrew Davies points out, Jane is often misunderstood: 'I think the reader is swayed by views of Jane which are not Austen's but are in fact Emma's, whose bad judgment is notorious. For example, Frank Churchill, who is a total liar and someone you can trust only so far as you can throw, is seen quite favourably by Emma for most of the story.'

Jane's reserve, in fact, comes from having to keep secret her engagement to Frank. Given Frank's subsequent attentions to Emma and her eager reciprocation, it isn't surprising that Emma is the last person in Highbury for whom Jane would feel friendship. 'I think Jane Fairfax is a very passionate woman in a very awkward situation,' says Andrew. 'My evidence for that is her extraordinary musical talent which everybody admires, and her predilection for Italian songs, which I think is perhaps her only way of expressing the desperate situation that she's in. Here's somebody who would love to be open but can't be.' So, when Emma and Jane sing at Randalls, Andrew suggested that Emma plays a simple pretty tune, while Jane chooses a more passionate Italian one. In this way, the audience has the opportunity to see that Jane is potentially a more interesting and complex character than Emma will allow.

The character who created the most discussion at the scripting stage was Frank Churchill. We were all agreed that Frank must arrive on the scene as an extremely charming and appropriate suitor for Emma. He is the only man she has even remotely considered as a match for herself, and his father and Mrs Weston would clearly love to see them get together. Only Knightley sees him as a 'trifling silly' fellow but, as we learn, his views on Frank are partly due to his feelings of jealousy. When Frank and Jane's engagement is finally revealed, it is clear that Frank is a dreadful deceiver. But how harshly should we judge him? Our first instincts were to try to excuse him. His was a dreadful predicament, if he had announced his engagement he would probably have been disinherited. Flirting with Emma seemed to him to be the safest way to hide the engagement, behaviour that he felt was justifiable because he didn't see any signs that Emma was in love with him. He does seem to take more pleasure in sustaining these deceptions than mere necessity would require, and his teasing and belittling of Jane to Emma appeared to show an inexplicably crueller streak, but we, like most of Highbury, wanted to forgive him. Andrew, however, argued strongly that Frank did not deserve such a sympathetic response. 'Frank Churchill is both disturbed and dangerous in my view. His mother went and died on him and his father handed him over to his aunt, who has treated him appallingly, so he really has it in for women. He plays to them. I think he's a clever, dangerous misogynistic charmer – dangerous because he's taken the trouble to work out how girls' minds work. He treats Emma badly, but he treats Jane worse because he is terrified of Jane's power over him. He just *has* to be in control of the game.'

Consequently, Andrew wrote a scene into the final sequence at Donwell in which Emma goes over to Jane to apologize for her past behaviour and they quickly forgive each other. But Frank's behaviour

Frank is a 'clever, dangerous, misogynistic charmer' (Andrew Davies).

is still disturbing. Now that their engagement is public, the game-playing is no longer necessary, but Frank can't stop. He talks to Emma about Jane's skin and 'the turn of her throat' in a stage whisper so that Jane cannot help but hear him and be made to feel uncomfortable. He enjoys her embarrassment. 'I think she's going to have a sad marriage,' comments Andrew. 'She's a sophisticated girl who's absolutely crazy about a shallow man and she knows it.' We see that Emma gains this insight into their relationship at the end of the film, although in the book she's more prepared to forgive him.

THE DETECTIVE STORY

The arrival of Jane Fairfax and Frank Churchill in Highbury kicks off one of the most hidden sub-plots in fiction. 'I don't think there's a chance of people getting the detective story, or even realizing there's a lot of clues being dropped, on the first reading of the book because they don't know it's a detective story,' says Andrew. 'Jane Austen never told anybody! So you have to read the book twice to get all the clues.' For the adaptation, Andrew had to look at ways to give the audience a fair chance of picking up those clues, without giving too much away.

Knightley surveys his harvested fields.

'Somebody gave Jane Fairfax a piano,' says Andrew. 'That's the only starting point you've got. It's a mystery because Jane doesn't appear to know who sent it. So I decided to make more of this by actually showing it being delivered. I'm surprised Jane Austen didn't have anything to say about how they got this big piano into the Bates' tiny set of rooms above a shop. I think it had to be one of those things with a hoist and pulley, which would have been the talk of the village.'

It's an extraordinarily generous gift and so, not surprisingly, everyone in Highbury speculates as to who sent the piano, except Jane who appears reticent in offering her own opinion. Many think it must be from the man who raised her, Colonel Campbell, but Emma suspects it is from a Mr Dixon, the Colonel's son-in-law, who Emma knows saved Jane from drowning in a boating accident. Frank encourages Emma in this view. 'I think people who are used to genre detective television would have worked out that it couldn't be from Mr Dixon or Colonel Campbell because they are offstage characters whom we never meet, which would make it very boring,' says Andrew. 'So it has to be either Knightley or Frank Churchill, if you're really paying attention.'

By the time of the strawberry picking sequence, Andrew felt the audience should be starting to guess more about the secret relationship between Frank and Jane. By now, Emma no longer considers Frank as a romantic possibility for herself, and so our interest in him has changed focus. 'I wrote in a little scene in which Jane, hurrying away from Donwell, meets Frank in the distance and they seem to argue. No one but the audience sees this.' At the Box Hill picnic the next day, Knightley observes the strange behaviour between Jane and Frank and, believing Emma to be in love with Frank, tries unsuccessfully to caution her.

We, the audience, however, will have reason to be more suspicious. When the secret engagement is discovered soon after, it should come as a full realization of what we were beginning to suspect, rather than as something completely out of the blue.

SOCIAL CONTEXT

'Although we were squeezed for space I wanted to give some weight to the social context of the story; to say something about the world these people live in,' comments Andrew. He chose to start the film with an incidental detail from the book: the image of a group of chicken thieves breaking into the Woodhouse's poultry house. On the way to Miss Taylor's wedding the next morning, Mr Woodhouse is unsettled by the break-in and wonders how safe his world is. We should not forget that the French Revolution is still very recent history to Mr Woodhouses' generation. As they ride to the church, they pass tumbledown cottages that aren't fit for habitation, but we see families in them. '*I* would have been in one of those cottages,' says Andrew, 'and so would most of the audience. I think it's an interesting aspect of this book, the fears and evasions of the aristocracy and gentry, living in such close proximity to the great unwashed.'

The story of Robert Martin also gives valuable context for our main characters. A yeoman farmer on Knightley's estate, Robert Martin seems a perfect match for Harriet. But Emma judges Robert to be not much better than a peasant, though she is entirely ignorant of how he lives. Despite the difficulties of squeezing everything into two hours, everyone agreed that it was important to keep the sequence where Harriet and Emma visit the Martins' farm. Director Diarmuid Lawrence says, 'The house is very pleasant; most of us would be very happy to settle somewhere in Wiltshire in a house like that.' We are led to realize that Emma's view of Robert is misguided and that he is in fact in a very comfortable and respectable position. Later in the film, Andrew wrote in a scene where we see Robert Martin and Knightley helping to bring in the harvest; a scene designed to underscore the sense of community. 'I thought it would be nice to think of Knightley as a person whose authority was so secure that he could roll up his sleeves and join in with the men,' says Andrew. This sequence culminates in the end of the film with Knightley hosting a harvest supper which brings the entire community together. *(See Chapter 5 for a full discussion of the script-to-screen process of the harvest supper.)*

Cottages unfit for habitation.

Harriet leaves after her visit to the Martins' farmhouse.

CHAPTER 2

The cast

ONE of the key decisions made about the casting for *Emma* was to be as true to the book as possible in terms of the ages of the characters. In the novel Emma is just 21. Harriet Smith is only 17. Jane Fairfax is the same age as Emma, though perhaps more mature. Frank is 23 years old. Mr Elton is about 26, a little younger than his new bride, Augusta, though she often behaves as if she were middle-aged. This decision meant finding a number of very young actors who were experienced enough to carry large and challenging parts.

'This is the most difficult aspect of casting an Austen or a Brontë or many of the classic books,' says casting director Janey Fothergill. 'The heroines are always beautiful 21-year-olds who have to carry the whole story. There just aren't that many of them to choose from. Emma, for example, is described as rich, beautiful and 21. She's strong and likes to be in control. It'd be difficult to find any actress in real life that you could so describe, who has the class and the right period feel.

'Kate Beckinsale, in fact, does have a lot of these qualities already and makes you believe she has the rest,' says Janey. 'She has a great confidence, is very intelligent and is aware of the fact that she's good-looking and well-spoken. She has a real sense of herself, and in that way is probably not too dissimilar from Emma. At least, I'm sure she's near enough to be able to understand Emma very well.'

Casting Harriet was equally difficult. 'There aren't that many girls who look like a genuinely innocent 17-year-old and yet have enough acting experience to carry such a large part,' says Janey. 'Samantha Morton is a one-off. She is both very experienced and very talented and is only 18 herself. She and Kate looked right together.'

Harriet 'was a very pretty girl, and her beauty happened to be of a sort which Emma particularly admired. She was short and fair, with a fine bloom, blue eyes, light hair, regular features, and a look of great sweetness' (Jane Austen).

15

Mrs Bates 'was a very old lady, almost past everything but tea and quadrille. She lived with her single daughter in a very small way, and was considered with all the regard and respect which a harmless old lady under such untoward circumstances can excite'
(Jane Austen).

Knightley is meant to be 16 years older than Emma. Given that Kate looks a young 21, it was decided to go for a Knightley closer to 35 than to 40. Director Diarmuid Lawrence wanted a Knightley who had vigour and dynamism, and didn't appear to be just a stuffed shirt. 'Knightley's a gentleman with grace and authority, a man who's comfortable with himself,' say Diarmuid. 'But what's quite delightful about Mark Strong's interpretation is that he is also able to get quietly into a juvenile rage about Frank Churchill, who triggers all his male responses of competition. This is a wonderfully human quality I think.'

Frank Churchill is a particularly complex character to play. He must be charming, energetic and handsome, but he is also cruel and potentially dangerous. The actor must take care not to 'play the end'. The audience, like all Highbury, has to be charmed and delighted by Frank at first. 'It's quite a small field of actors who can play all this, be charismatic and handsome and look just 23,' comments Diarmuid. 'There were a couple of serious contenders, but in the end we went for Raymond Coulthard, who was the best actor.'

Despite the number of young leads needed for the film, *Emma* also has some choice older parts, in Mr Woodhouse, Miss Bates, and the Westons. 'There are a lot of very distinguished actors who are very keen to do this kind of work,' says Janey. 'Even if it's just a few scenes, you can attract top talent if you have a classy script and cast. It makes such a difference to the overall quality of a film. The great benefit of having an experienced older cast is that they often have a very settling influence on the younger actors, who are usually very jittery. Even though the younger ones may have done a few feature films, they simply don't have the experience of people like Prunella Scales, Bernard Hepton, Samantha Bond or James Hazeldine. Actors of that calibre always have a positive effect on the whole cast.'

'I never in my life saw a man more intent on being agreeable than Mr Elton. With men he can be rational and unaffected, but when he has ladies to please, every feature works'
(John Knightley).

'The quarter of an hour quite convinced her [Emma] that Mrs Elton was a vain woman, extremely well satisfied with herself, and thinking much of her own importance ... that, if not foolish, she was ignorant' (Jane Austen).

Mr Woodhouse 'was a much older man in ways than in years ... He was a nervous man, easily depressed; fond of everybody that he was used to, and hating to part with them; hating change of every kind' (Jane Austen).

'Mr Perry, the apothecary, was an intelligent, gentleman-like man, whose frequent visits were one of the comforts of Mr Woodhouse's life' (Jane Austen).

'Mr Weston was a man of unexceptionable character, easy fortune, suitable age, and pleasant manners' (Jane Austen).

Mrs Weston was 'a friend and companion such as few possessed, intelligent, well-informed, useful, gentle, knowing all the ways of the family' (Jane Austen).

'Emma Woodhouse, handsome, clever, and rich, with a comfortable home and happy disposition, seemed to unite some of the best blessings of existence; and had lived nearly twenty-one years in the world with little to vex her' (Jane Austen).

KATE BECKINSALE ON PLAYING EMMA

People tend to have very strong opinions about Emma – that she's bossy and insufferable – but I've always liked her. I could never see what people complained about, I thought she was marvellous. She seems to me to behave in a perfectly reasonable way, though I've become cagey about drawing parallels between Emma and myself. But I can certainly remember times at school when I've pushed friends into doing this or that, which could probably be seen as bullying. Of couse, at the time I felt completely justified. I suppose this is how Emma treats Harriet; she feels that you have to be cruel to be kind. She might be misguided in this but she never acts out of malice; she thinks she knows what's best for Harriet and is determined to make it happen.

I think a lot of her interference comes from boredom. It could have been a tragic story. Of course, she's wealthy, has a beautiful home and is well-loved by her family, but remember: her mother died when she was three and she's left with a father and sister who constantly sit in corners whinging about their imagined illnesses. Then her sister marries and she, at thirteen, takes on the responsibility for Hartfield and an old father. She has no company of her own age and certainly there's no one to match her intellectually. She's not been allowed to travel even as far as Box Hill, which is only six miles away.

It's like having all the most wonderful presents at Christmas, but no batteries. So she makes herself focus on the wrappings and boxes. She decides, though I don't think consciously, to make the best of it. I think it's something people do when there doesn't seem to be a way out of a situation. She seems to think: 'Oh, I'm fine. I'm never poorly. Everything's marvellous. I'm very happy. Poor everyone else who isn't me.' This is her way of coping and I admire her for that. But she has so much energy, it has to be channelled somewhere or she'd go out of her mind with boredom. This is where her match-making and her interference come from. She has a vivid imagination and too much time to fill.

Knightley is the only one who can equal her but, of course, there's a 16-year age gap which, when you're a child, is a lot. She sees him every day, they are good friends, she's comfortable with him and enjoys the attention. She's missed out on all the teenage crushes; there's been no one with whom she can flirt. Frank Churchill is the first potential suitor and, though she's keen to see if she'll fall in love with him, she quickly decides that he's 'not necessary to her happiness'. I think this is because she's sort-of in love with Knightley all the time, though she doesn't realize it until the end. It's only when she thinks, mistakenly, that he's about to marry Harriet that the shock of this makes her *know* that she loves him.

It's odd how I was asked to play the part. I'd been to audition when I was in the middle of moving flats so I didn't have a permanent address. One night I was at the stage door of the National Theatre waiting for a friend to finish his performance when a package was delivered for him. I sat with this on my knee for half an hour. When he arrived he said: 'Actually, it's been sent to me to give to you.' I opened it and it was the script with a letter asking me to play Emma. It was all quite a shock. I was very, very pleased, but nervous. The part requires such faithfulness and love. It was a big responsibility.

The character's so well drawn in the book. She doesn't feel stuffy or old-fashioned. Some of it is surprisingly modern.

Kate learns how to check the camera lens to see that it's clean.

Not so the language! It seemed easy when reading it on the page. It's very close to the way we speak, but that's the trouble with it. If it were Shakespeare you'd start by knowing it was difficult and you'd think: 'I can get in and attack this'. But Jane Austen's is difficult and deceptive. Close it may be to the way we speak, but not close enough to be able to feel comfortable with it immediately. The sentences can be very long with the sense coming right at the end. You worry that people will have switched off before you can get to the end of one! You start by feeling very stilted and can't work out why. Then you get the rhythm of it and it begins to feel normal. We were all very cheered by reading that the *Pride and Prejudice* cast had found it difficult too!

The dancing was great fun. I did a lot of dancing as a child and love it, but I always pretend I'm a hopeless dancer, then the choreographer will think I've had to struggle hard. Singing, on the other hand, is my least favourite thing to do in public (except for being naked). It made me as anxious as if I'd been asked to do a nude scene. I sat at the piano thinking: 'This can't happen. Someone will save me, someone will say: "We've changed our minds – you don't have to sing after all."' And then you have to do a terrible rehearsal in front of the film crew and actors all of whom, you imagine, have probably been in Sondheim musicals and this weedy little voice comes out. But when you have to do something that you desperately don't want to do and you manage to do it, it's really good for you. My one consolation was that Emma isn't supposed to be brilliant – that would have finished me off.

Now having played Emma I still like her very much. I love the way she thunderbolts her way through life. I feel she does have her moments of regret, thinking that everything she's done is dreadful, that she's behaved abominably. But her spirit is never crushed.

MARK STRONG ON PLAYING KNIGHTLEY

At the time I was offered the part, I was at the Royal Court, playing a homeless down-and-out from Yorkshire. So the part of Knightley came completely out of left field. I had read *Emma* in school but I didn't like it much at the time. Now, I realize that I didn't understand the ironic tone. So, coming back to it was lovely. It was also very exciting because I'd never played that kind of a character before. Knightley's a man, a mature man. That's what attracted me.

It's not a love story in the way that, say, *Pride and Prejudice* is. But a lot of people said to me, 'Oh, it's the Darcy part,' which it isn't at all. Then a friend I spoke to who had read *Emma* at university said 'Oh, you're playing boring old Knightley.' And I know what he meant, reading it as a teenager you feel like this man is set up as 'Mr Goody' or 'Mr Establishment'. So I had to go back and find out who this man really was.

Jane Austen doesn't give that many clues in the book as to his character. Other characters in the book say a lot about him and it's *all*

'Mr Knightley's air is so remarkably good ... You might not see one in a hundred with gentleman so plainly written as in Mr Knightley'
(Emma).

good. What I found underneath, however, was a man desperately struggling with his emotions. For example, there's a scene where he gets really annoyed because Frank Churchill has gone all the way to London to get his hair cut. It's a witty scene, and you put Knightley's behaviour down to his being an older kind of guy who sees that as foppishness. But it suddenly came to life for me when I realized it is his jealousy of Frank that is motivating him. This is something I just didn't glean from the book the first time I read it.

I pared it down to basics. He's loved Emma for a long time, though he's not necessarily conscious that he wants to marry her at the beginning of the story. He is patient and he's waiting and he's guiding her, and then suddenly here comes this boy, Frank Churchill, who ruins everything. Knightley's whole world is turned on its head. I think the first time he feels that everything is falling away is when he and Emma walk into the Westons' party together. We have this lovely chat – she's smiling and I'm smiling – and then the door opens and there's Frank, and she beams a big smile at him. Suddenly it's not about me and her anymore. I think he feels a bit superfluous, and I must admit in playing the scene, that I felt a bit like a spare part too. He gets so irritated by this boy, and starts telling off Emma more sharply than he's ever done before. He's probably going home in the evening and thinking, 'Why on Earth did I do that? What is happening?' I think, slowly, he works it out for himself. He comes to realize that he loves her. And he fears that he may lose her to this young pup.

At this point I worried that, because I was always having a go at Emma, the audience might not see the love behind it. I was talking to Jimmy Hazeldine about this one day and he said not to worry, that for him the scene on Box Hill where Knightley pulls Emma up on her behaviour to Miss Bates was an act of love. He said that people don't take that kind of interest in somebody unless they have very strong feelings for them.

After that scene, Knightley is so convinced that he's lost Emma to Frank that he takes himself off to London and only returns when he hears of Frank's engagement to Jane. What's lovely about the proposal scene is that it sort of happens by accident. He thinks she'll be devastated about Frank. She thinks he is in love with Harriet. So neither expects what suddenly happens. I loved filming that scene even though it was shot in the first week. I think it gave it an edge that perhaps might not have been there had we done it later. I remember realizing at the end of the first week that I'd already shot the proposal and the big row with Emma over Robert Martin, which were my two biggest scenes. From then on it got easier.

Mark and Kate keep fit between shots.

ACTORS' IMPRESSIONS

Raymond Coulthard:

I was invited to Janey's office for a chat about *Emma*. I arrived in the West End with 15 minutes to spare and, as I didn't know the story at all, popped quickly into a bookshop. This was not to look at a copy of the novel (which, with only 15 minutes spare, would have been useless) but to find one of those life-saving publications called York Notes, which everyone wrongly assumes were written for struggling A level students. They were, of course, written for actors who haven't had time to read the novel for which they are about to audition. Within a few minutes I had rapidly run through the list of characters and my instinct said that if I were offered a part in this, I would want it to be Frank Churchill. I met Janey and she told me they were looking for – yes, you've guessed it – Frank Churchill. Providence prevailed.

Prunella Scales:

Having recorded *Emma* twice for audio cassette and once for radio, I jumped at the chance of playing Miss Bates, but then was horribly disappointed to find that the part had been savagely cut to about a tenth of its original content. Despite the verbal extravagance of the character, Jane Austen did use her to drop clues about the plot. However, in an adaptation that must reduce the book to 100 minutes of screen time, garrulousness must be sacrificed to function.

My first television job ever was a black-and-white serial of *Pride and Prejudice* with Peter Cushing as Darcy. We did it live, in the studio, tripping over cables as we rushed between sets and changed costumes behind flats. Milton Rosmer, an actor of the Old School playing Mr Bennett, said, 'Let me give you a tip, my dear. On television, always touch the person you're talking to, that way you'll never put yourself out of shot.' The main note I had from Diarmuid on *Emma* however, was 'Don't worry, my darling, you're not in shot.' Story of my life?

Olivia Williams:

I was invited to audition for the part of Jane Fairfax who is supposed to have a beautiful voice.

Janey Fothergill's office is no more than a large cupboard but it contains three filing cabinets, a desk, a sofa and a photocopier. I was asked to sing an eighteenth century Italian song. Diarmuid was perching on a cardboard box in the corner and Sue was flattened against the filing cabinets. The sound I produced was like a Land Rover parking on gravel. I realized they had a fine view of my fillings. Handy tip: avoid shouting during exciting football matches the night before singing auditions.

'Mr John Knightley was a tall, gentlemanlike, and very clever man ... domestic and respectable in his private character; but with reserved manners which prevented him being generally pleasing; and capable of being sometimes out of humour' (Jane Austen).

Robert Martin 'is an excellent young man, both as son and brother ... [his] manners have sense, sincerity, and good-humour to recommend them' (Knightley).

The leading men put their 'best foot forward'.

CAST BIOGRAPHIES

Kate Beckinsale
(Emma Woodhouse)
played the part of Hero in
Kenneth Branagh's *Much
Ado About Nothing*. She
was Flora Poste in the
BBC adaptation of *Cold
Comfort Farm*. Her theatre
work has included a
national tour of *The
Seagull*, as Nina and *Clocks
and Whistles* at the Bush
Theatre. She starred as
Toni in *Sweetheart* for the
Royal Court Theatre.

Mark Strong
(Knightley) trained at the
Bristol Old Vic Theatre
School. He has worked for
the RSC, the National
Theatre and the Royal
Court Theatre. He played
the part of Tosker Cox in
the BBC drama *Our
Friends in the North* and
was David Lacey in
Between the Lines. His film
work includes *Fever Pitch*,
Century, *One Against the
Wind*, and *Captives*.

**Samantha
Morton**
(Harriet Smith) has been
acting since she was a child
through her involvement
with Central's Television
Workshop. She played
Tracy in two series of *Band
of Gold*. Her stage debut
was at the Royal Court
Upstairs in *Ashes and Sand*
and more recently in *Star-
Gazey Pie and Sauerkraut*.

**Raymond
Coulthard**
(Frank Churchill) trained at
the Bristol Old Vic
Theatre School. His
television work includes
two series of *Luv* for the
BBC, *Band of Gold*, *Castles*
and *Rhodes*. He played the
part of Young Scrooge in
Jim Henson's *The Muppet
Christmas Carol*, and starred
in Anthony Minghella's
The English Patient.

Bernard Hepton
(Mr Woodhouse). His
major television credits
include *The Scarlet
Pimpernel*, *Mansfield Park*,
Bleak House and *The Old
Devils*. His theatre credits
include *Hedda Gabler* and
The Taming of the Shrew at
the Bristol Old Vic
Theatre. He has appeared
in the films *Ghandi*, *Get
Carter*, *The Six Wives of
Henry VIII* and *Barry
Lyndon*.

Prunella Scales
(Miss Bates) has had a long
and distinguished career in
film and theatre. Her tele-
vision credits include
Fawlty Towers, *After Henry*,
The Rector's Wife and *When
We Are Married*. Prunella
has appeared in the films
An Awfully Big Adventure,
Howards End, *Chorus of
Disapproval* and *The Lonely
Passion of Judith Herne*.

James Hazeldine
(Mr Weston) has enjoyed
seasons at the RSC, the
National Theatre and the
Royal Court, where he has
appeared in *Troilus and
Cressida*, *Small Change* and
Crete and Sergeant Pepper.
He played Bayleaf in *Lon-
don's Burning*. As a director,
James has staged a national
tour of *Absent Friends* and
also directed *Heartbeat*,
London's Burning and *The
Knock*. for television.

Samantha Bond
(Mrs Weston) trained at the
Bristol Old Vic Theatre
School. She recently
appeared in the West End
in Edward Albee's *Three
Tall Women*. She was in *A
Winter's Tale* for the RSC
and *Les Liaisons
Dangereuses*. Her television
credits include *Poirot*,
Inspector Morse and
Mansfield Park. She played
the part of Ms Money-
penny in *Golden Eye*.

Lucy Robinson
(Mrs Elton) was Kim in *All Quiet on the Preston Front* and Mrs Hurst in *Pride and Prejudice*. Her theatre work includes the role of Daphne in the West End production of *Present Laughter*, directed by Tom Conti, and Celine in *The Hypochondriac* at the West Yorkshire Playhouse.

Dominic Rowan
(Mr Elton) trained at the Central School of Speech and Drama. His theatre work includes *The Rivals*, *Charlie's Aunt* and *Look Back in Anger*, all at The Royal Exchange, Manchester. For the BBC, Dominic has been in *The Tenant of Wildfell Hall*, *No Bananas*, *Devil's Advocate* and *Between the Lines*.

Olivia Williams
(Jane Fairfax) graduated from the Bristol Old Vic Theatre School in 1991. She has worked for the RSC, where her roles have included Lydia in *Misha's Party* and Mrs Friendall in *The Wives Excuse*. Olivia's television work includes *Van Der Valk* and *The Ruth Rendell Mysteries*. She has starred in the film *Wesley – A Brand from the Burning*.

Alistair Petrie
(Robert Martin) trained at the London Academy of Music and Dramatic Art. He played Herbert Pocket in the Theatre Clwyd production of *Great Expectations* and Jolyon in *No Flies on Mister Hunter*, directed by Janet Suzman at the Chelsea Centre. He has appeared on television in *All Quiet on the Preston Front*, *Demob* and *Scarlet and Black*.

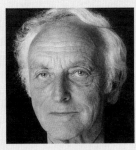

Guy Henry
(John Knightley) has worked at the RSC and the National Theatre. His theatre credits include *Hamlet*, *The Venetian Twins* and *Twelfth Night*. His performance of Ananias in *The Alchemist* was nominated for an Olivier Award for Best Comedy Performance. For television, Guy has appeared in *Stay Lucky*, *Spywatch*, *Rumpole of the Bailey*, *The Two of Us* and *Family Ties*.

Dido Miles
(Isabella Knightley) trained at the Royal Academy of Dramatic Art. Since leaving she has played the part of Dinah in the Warner Bros. feature film *Black Beauty*. She has also appeared in *First Knight*. She was Louise Abbott in *The Bill* and has also worked on *Frontiers*, *Casualty*, *London Bridge* and *Permanent Red*.

Peter Howell
(Mr Perry) appeared in an early BBC version of *Pride and Prejudice*, *The Mill on the Floss* and *The Brothers*. He has worked on numerous comedy shows, and played the part of Duncan Cheesewright in *Jeeves and Wooster*. Peter's film credits include *The Innocent Sleep*, *Princess Caribou* and *Shadowlands*.

Sylvia Barter
(Mrs Bates) has worked extensively for the BBC, appearing in *Love Hurts*, *When the Boat Comes In*, *No Place Like Home* and *Casualty*. She also starred in Channel 4's *Porterhouse Blue*. A West End run of *Waltz of the Toreadors* and *Absolute Hell* at the National Theatre are among Sylvia's many theatre credits.

CHAPTER 3

The design

FINDING HIGHBURY

'The village of Highbury was the most important location to find,' says production designer Don Taylor. 'You can build sets for specific rooms but, if you want a whole village, it's got to have a real life to it.'

Diarmuid wanted to be able to shoot round 360 degrees: 'There's a big scene where Emma shows Frank Churchill the sights of Highbury. There's no excuse for not showing the town there. I wanted them to be able to walk anywhere which, of course, can cause problems for a location manager.'

Sue Quinn was the location manager who had to find it: 'I talked at length with Don about what Highbury should look like; whether we should stick to the script, where it's set in Surrey, which would have been red brick. It's generally thought that Jane Austen had Leatherhead or Cobham in mind as Highbury but one couldn't find what one needed there nowadays.

'Highbury to me should be an overgrown village, with quite a few shops. Most small towns then would have been linear, just one long street. More than one main street and it would have been seen as a big town for that period. It had to be a country town but that gave us problems, as the story happens over four seasons and we could only shoot for six weeks during mid-summer. So we had to find somewhere where lush fields and trees were not too apparent.

'When I saw Lacock, I thought: "This is it. We could change this back to 1813 quite quickly and it would be cost effective." It's a National Trust village so there are no television aerials and what there was of the twentieth century could easily be disguised.

OPPOSITE AND ABOVE: *Filming in Lacock.*

Sue Quinn.

The red brick-house before the false front is added.

Miss Bates 'was interested in everybody's happiness; quick-sighted to everybody's merits; thought herself ... surrounded with blessings in ... so many good neighbours and friends' (Jane Austen).

'Although Lacock had in the past had an excellent experience of filming with *Pride and Prejudice* in 1994, when we approached them about *Emma*, the village had just been through a disastrous time with another film crew and were, understandably, anxious. We decided to have a public meeting to explain our requirements and answer questions. Afterwards, every house was written to and then visited and, in the end, we were warmly welcomed.'

DEMANDS OF THE SCRIPT

In Andrew's screenplay, there is a scene where a piano is delivered to Miss Bates' house (which is a first floor apartment over a shop) and it has to be hoisted by pulley through the window. It was clear that we wouldn't be allowed to remove an original window to do this, so it was decided to build a false façade over an existing house in Lacock. There would be a scaffolding skeleton and platform inside on which Prunella Scales could perch for all the scenes where Miss Bates accosts people from her window, which we would make removable. All the interior scenes would then be filmed in a built set in the studios. The ideal house proved to be the home of Susan Walker since it overlooked the site we'd chosen to recreate the old Market Cross. This would become the hub of Highbury life over which Miss Bates could keep constant watch. Susan Walker was very obliging and moved

into the home of her neighbour, Elsie Hunt, during the construcion work.

The other essential elements of Highbury were the Crown Inn exterior, the coaching inn and the forge by the market cross, Ford's haberdashery shop, the church and the outside of Mr Elton's vicarage. All of these we found in Lacock, though the interior church scenes we shot in Mildenhall church, which had last been refurbished in 1816 and was perfect for our needs.

CONVERTING LACOCK TO HIGHBURY

In the weeks before filming, deals had to be negotiated with all the businesses that would lose trade during filming. Each householder had to be approached about letting us change their curtains or door-knockers, possibly putting film lights in their front windows and what arrangements would be made for parking their cars.

We scheduled three days filming as necessary to complete all the scenes there. We knew we'd have to fit in with village events. Lacock is a popular tourist attraction so we agreed not to film or do preparation work during the weekends, which is their busiest time.

We had arranged to erect Miss Bates' house during the week before filming. As it only involved one small area, it would cause minimal disruption. To 'dress' the rest of the street and to lay the ground cover (which would transport the street back 150 years) would take two days. Obviously no one wanted this down longer than was necessary, so we agreed to start this process on the Monday. This would mean filming could start on Wednesday and be finished by the weekend. But we then heard that the annual flower show was to be held on Friday and the organizers needed access to the church from 4 p.m. on Thursday. It seemed we had three and a half days in which to cram six days' work. Diarmuid agreed to move part of one scene to a different location later in the shoot and to simplify the shots at the vicarage. Don and his construction manager, Roger Wilkins, planned the rest like a military exercise and decided they and the ground-cover team could work alongside each other and do the conversion in just one day.

Before the Westons run down the path to their wedding carriage, a carpet is unrolled to deaden the sound of their feet on gravel.

BELOW: *Lacock's own market cross outside the school (left) and reproduced in wood and polystyrene for filming in Church Street (right). Designer Don Taylor (centre).*

ABOVE: *Lacock moves back to 1815 (from left to right): Church Street 1996. The materials are delivered. The terram lining is cut to fit the street. Drains are covered with wire in case of rain. Earth and grit cover the lining.*

BELOW: *Jo adds final ground cover: a scattering of autumn leaves and a handful of horse manure. John Bush fills troughs with straw for horses, while Dempsey turns The Carpenter's Arms into the Bell Inn.*

THE WORK BEGINS

Erecting the façade of Miss Bates' house was a big job, almost like building a real one. It was pre-constructed in pieces in the workshop and transported to Lacock on the previous Wednesday. It took three days to put it together, paint it and put in the windows.

On Friday, the National Trust allowed us to paint all the window frames in the street, and the house owners let us change their curtains. Getting ahead in this way helped enormously, as we knew Monday would be frantic. During the weekend we disappeared leaving only a security guard to watch over Miss Bates' house as visitors, not believing it wasn't real, had taken to chipping bits off to test!

At eight o'clock on Monday morning, the team started to lay the ground cover. It was a large area to treat and so was done in two separate parts and took until 9.30 p.m. Meanwhile the design team worked alongside: dressing the street, changing signs, erecting the market cross, creating the forge, changing street furniture, disguising and camouflaging out-of-period flowers. Droves of tourists turned up to watch, which compounded all the problems, but the weather was wonderful and a holiday mood grew in spite of all the hectic work that had to be completed for filming to start at 8 a.m. on the following day.

ABOVE: *(left to right) The pieces of Miss Bates' house arrive and are assembled on a scaffolding frame.*

BELOW: *The final touches: windows are put in and beams painted (left). The completed house during filming (right).*

ABOVE: *Crane shot for the night arrival at the Crown Inn dance.* BELOW: *The lighting team keeps an eye on the sun (left). Diarmuid rehearses Frank and Emma's walk around Highbury (right).*

At eleven o'clock on Wednesday night the main film unit finished, leaving Thursday and Friday for everything to be returned to normal. Our experience of filming in Lacock was, once again, a very happy one and we are grateful for the warm welcome we received. We were also delighted to hear that the flower show was a great success and raised £2,500 for the church.

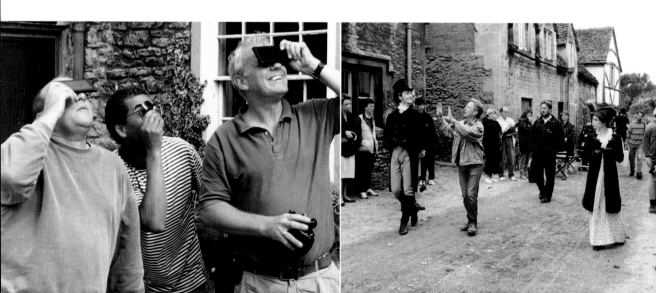

FILMING IN THE STUDIO: INTERIOR BATES' HOUSE

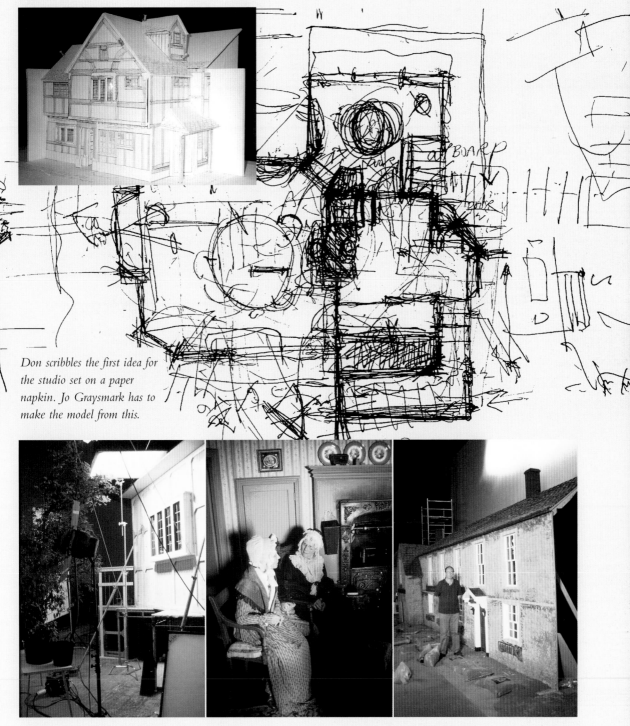

Don scribbles the first idea for the studio set on a paper napkin. Jo Graysmark has to make the model from this.

Miss and Mrs Bates in their sitting room: from one window they see a garden (branches tied to lighting stands), from the other, a view across the street in Highbury (here built to half-size to give correct perspective).

HARTFIELD

Diarmuid wanted to put into an audience's mind very early on the particular circumstances of how Emma lives: 'Hartfield has to be big to make that point. It should feel elegant, but there shouldn't be too many cosy corners; it is a house that is much too large for two people, particularly when one of them is a healthy 21-year-old woman and the other is a querulous old man who's never happier than when he's sitting by a large fire.'

Don looked at many houses and ended up in Wiltshire, just outside Salisbury: 'My first thought on seeing Trafalgar Park was how wonderful the red brick would look against the snow. It was a very exciting image. We'd seen beautiful houses in Cotswold stone, but I felt it couldn't have the same impact as it would against this magnificent red brick. The garden was lovely too, with a wonderful sense of symmetry, which is so important with Jane Austen. It was classical and elegant and stylish.

'Inside we wanted it to look sophisticated, but to give the impression that little had altered since Emma's mother had died eighteen years earlier. Mr Woodhouse is notoriously distressed by change of any sort, so it had to refer back to an earlier age whilst still showing a confidence and good taste.

THE JOINED-TOGETHER
LOCATION PHOTOGRAPHS OF
TRAFALGAR PARK:
ABOVE: *the formal gardens.
Planting will be changed to reflect
the seasons.*
LEFT: *The magnificent entrance
hall.*

*Jo puts the final touches to the front
door.*

'One advantage for us was that the main rooms at Trafalgar Park were completely empty so it gave us a free hand. The drawing-room had been painted yellow, but we decided to go for a grey-green colour which would give the actors and costumes more of a chance to dominate. We always went for subtle colours. Perhaps, if we'd have been showing Mrs Elton's new decoration, it might have been different, but all the interiors we see belong to characters with taste. Colours have to be chosen that will let people be seen. It's like a white landscape in a way, but obviously more subtle. Design, costumes and the lighting are all taking it in turns to be the "white landscape", each department playing with light, colours, fabrics, so that the actors and the text come through, rather than the design itself.'

BELOW: *The main drawing-room
in its original colour (left) and
repainted for filming (right).*

Sudeley Castle and the ruins.

DONWELL ABBEY

'The house was larger than Hartfield, and totally unlike it, covering a good deal of ground, rambling and irregular ... its ample gardens stretching down to meadows washed by a stream ... It was just what it ought to be, and looked what it was – and Emma felt an increasing respect for it as the residence of a family of such true gentility.'

This is Jane Austen's description of Donwell Abbey and Sue Quinn had to find it: 'I immediately thought of Sudely Castle, in Gloucestershire, because I knew it had ruins in the garden and sits quite beautifully in the rolling English countryside.'

But it was not quite as simple as that. It had to have a Great Hall, large enough to accommodate the final harvest supper scene, and a

The interiors of Stanway House felt exactly right for Knightley's home.

couple of rooms that could fit Andrew's script note: 'Emma comes in – it should feel cool and spacious inside – not daunting at all, despite its size, something of a bachelor's house. A big dog pads around after her. This is a nice place, she thinks. I like it here.'

Sue knew that the interiors of Sudely would be no good as it had been refurbished. 'But I felt that Stanway House, which is nearby and unchanged, would fit well for some of the interiors, though I knew the Great Hall there was too small. By now, we realized that the Donwell filming would be split over several locations.

'The brief for the hall was specific: it had to have a Medieval feel, be large enough for the long supper tables and the dancing that follows, have stone floors rather than wooden and a fire place where a whole beast could be roasted. Having found our exterior at Sudely, it was important that the hall would feel as if it belonged to the same house.

The Great Hall at Broughton Castle before filming (above) and with the pig roasting in the fireplace (below).

The raging storm off Weymouth (above) was filmed in a field in Oxfordshire (below).

'There are not many Great Halls of the size we needed without going to the vast stately homes, which would have had totally the wrong feel and, as usual, we couldn't afford to go too far afield. I remembered Broughton Castle, near to Banbury, where the stonework fits perfectly with Sudely and the hall is beautifully proportioned. As soon as we walked in, we knew we'd found the right place.'

The final element needed was the famous Donwell strawberry beds. We knew we would have to create these and that they could be made to work in any of the three locations we had so far chosen for Donwell. But it made economic sense to move as many scenes as possible within reach of London and we'd already decided to film several of our different locations in the house and grounds of Thame Park in Oxfordshire. Here we'd found the Hartfield dining-room, bedroom and painting studio, as well as the Martins' farm and house, the cottages of the rural poor, the gypsy camp and – even – the boat scene in the storm off Weymouth!

So we looked again at the derelict walled garden there. It was beautiful, but very neglected, needing months of work in a normal gardening calendar. But Don and his team took up the challenge: the weeds and brambles were cleared, the strawberry beds dug and grass pathways laid. The circles of box hedge were clipped back into shape and filled with flowers, the overgrown espalier fruit trees which lined the walls were pruned and the broken panes in the glass houses were covered with judicious planting. The gate was mended and an arch of rambling roses built over it. Finally, of course, the hundreds of strawberry plants were supplemented by dozens of boxes of the ripe fruit brought in from the local market.

ABOVE: *Thame Park's derelict walled garden is transformed into the Donwell strawberry beds.*

BELOW: *The entire camera recce team is needed to mark out the part of the field to be cut for the Donwell harvesting scene.*

SPRING

SUMMER

AUTUMN

WINTER

RANDALLS EXTERIOR AND INTERIOR

Diarmuid on Randalls:
*'We don't have time to tell the full
story of the Westons, so the location
must do a lot of this for us. Theirs
is a late and blissfully happy
marriage. The house should be cosy,
with the countryside right on the
doorstep. The Elizabethan house
seemed perfect: a place where this
delightful couple can sit by the fire
and think: "How lucky we are!".'*

THE CROWN INN

before

after

ABOVE: *Don: 'I deliberately went for reds and gold in the Crown Inn as I wanted to hit that room with a high of colour.'*

OPPOSITE: *Filming in summer means we have to cheat the seasons. The camera team dresses spring foliage into shot. Frances ties on silk roses. Remi shoots in harvest field. Security lights disguised with autumn leaves. Snow put down at Hartfield and Randalls.*

ABOVE: *Servants arrive with all the paraphernalia for the picnic (left) and carry it up the hill (right).*

BOX HILL

Finding the location

For Diarmuid the Box Hill picnic was a particular challenge: 'It's one of the most famous scenes in the book and I found the thought of having to get it right rather intimidating. Filming on the real Box Hill would be a disaster: it's knee-deep in visitors and no longer looks as it would have done 150 years ago.'

Sue Quinn: 'My brief was to find a chalk hill, covered in wild box or similar, which looked green and luscious. Diarmuid was also very clear that he wanted it to look as if it was a really steep climb. Of course, there are many such hills in England, but financial constraints meant it had to be near our studio base, which severely limited the choice.

'The hill in the Chilterns that was chosen fitted the bill though it did create some problems. The view couldn't be shot from all sides without a sighting of Didcot Power Station. The fact that the land was owned by three separate people complicated the negotiations, particularly when we had to make a last-minute decision to change our filming days to avoid bad weather. There was a sawmill at the bottom which had to be paid to stop work, though we were able to employ their four-wheel drive vehicles and drivers, as there was no other way of getting the equipment and the actors to the top.

'It's also a site of Scientific Interest in that the red kites being introduced into the countryside had decided to nest in that spot. Fortunately, the eggs had hatched, or we wouldn't have been allowed to film there.

BELOW: *After the picnic, the servants carry it all back down again (left).*
A gas-burner is placed in front of the camera to create the heat-haze effect (right).

'The major problem on the filming days was light aircraft. We'd been lucky with the weather but that inevitably means amateur pilots will take to the air in droves. The RAF will always co-operate and offer an exclusion zone, but this never works with flying clubs. In fact, when pilots see a film crew on a hill, they quite often do another few circuits to watch the fun and thus ensure that filming has to stop for even longer.'

The crew push the coach back into position.

THE SCENE

Diarmuid: 'When you analyse the sequence at Box Hill, you realize it breaks down into the arrival, getting up the hill, the anagram game, the picnic itself and the scene between Knightley and Emma as they leave. Important things happen here, and we had only two days scheduled to film all this. I was keen also to make a point about what a cavalcade it would take to get everyone and everything there.'

Andrew always wanted the audience to be aware of social divisions in Highbury society and this scene enabled us to see the work that such a picnic would create for the servants. Nine people decide to go on a trip to Box Hill. This involves coaches and coachmen, grooms, footmen, a luggage cart containing elaborate food, furniture and parasols, and the servants carry it all up the hill and then down again afterwards.

The cast try to stay cool while rehearsing in the full sun of Box Hill.

THE PICNIC:
Food stylist Debbie Brodie

Catering for the picnic was difficult because the same food had to appear over two days and the weather was very hot; on the first day the temperature was in the upper 80s and we were on the top of a very steep hill with no possibility of refrigeration. The ground was dry and we had a lot of sand blowing around. The director had asked for a particularly elaborate outside banquet at the top of the hill, to contrast with the simple picnic that the servants were eating at the bottom.

All the food had to be transported up over very rough ground in four-wheel drive vehicles that threw everything and everyone around in the process, so we had to make sure the large confections we'd constructed could survive the journey.

We cooked large cuts of meat (hams, turkeys, sides of beef) because the wealthy ate a lot of meat. I also prepared several dishes in aspic. There's this lovely recipe with quails that I'd been longing to make from John Farley's book, *The London Art of Cookery*, which was published in 1783. I set six little roasted quails in jelly with nasturtiams and parsley, which was very pretty, and layered cooked vegetables in aspic. We made a mould of summer fruits in the same way because you get a wonderful effect of light shining through the jewelled jelly colours. Dozens of sweet brioches, which are like profiteroles, were built into a pyramid and stuck together with cream and sugar, then decorated with frosted rose buds.

We made these colossal fruit pyramids, which are certainly *not* the thing to do when you've got four hundred-weight of food to put out and you're in a complete tiz. They take a very long time. You have to have a completely level base onto which you put a layer of the

BELOW: *Debbie builds a fruit pyramid (left) for the puddings table (right).*

larger fruits (apples, peaches, oranges). This you then spray with mounting glue and add a layer of leaves. I used Ivy leaves but you can use Vine or Bay leaves. Once that has dried, you do the next layer in the same way, with the fruits getting smaller as it gets higher. Any fruits can be used: cherries, strawberries, whatever takes your fancy. After the second layer, I spear down through the fruit with cocktail sticks to give extra strength. These dishes may have to be moved many times during the day and, though I wouldn't say you could drop one without it collapsing, they can certainly take some rough handling.

I'm sure people look at my cooking and think, 'Oh, she's gone too far this time'. But everything is based on fact. I use two really good Georgian cookery books by Hannah Glass and John Farley. Georgian food is quite lovely. The ingredients used were delicious, though, by today's standards, they were a bit heavy-handed with the cream, butter and eggs – up to 22 eggs in one cake! The poor kitchen maid would have had to stand and beat them all day, just for one cake. Obviously, labour was very cheap.

After filming, all the food is thrown away. Apart from the few pieces that the actors have to eat, none of it is made to be consumed. It's art work. The fruit tarts might look delicious but they're not. Often when we are filming in someone's house, I'm asked if I can leave something behind, but I wouldn't dream of it. The risk factor is too high. On one of my earlier films, I left the propmen to clear up. There was a half-cooked leg of pork that had been there for several days. The caretakers of the property took it for their dog but then decided to eat it themselves! Fortunately, no harm came to them but I've been terrified ever since and now make sure everything is destroyed.

CHAPTER 4

The costumes and make-up

COSTUME DESIGNER: *Jenny Beavan*

Having done *Sense and Sensiblity*, which was a joy, I was very much in two minds as to whether I should tackle another Jane Austen. But I thought the script for *Emma* was excellent and also the periods of the two are slightly different. *Sense and Sensibility* is placed in 1800 whereas *Emma* is set nearer to 1815. Quite a difference took place in those fifteen years from a design point of view. *Sense and Sensibility* costumes were very flowing and the lines were quite smooth but by the time of *Emma* you're beginning to get a bit of a peak on the shoulders and a little puff on the sleeves. The skirt length is somewhat shorter and more practical, its shape has become rather more triangular and you no longer get trains on the frocks. These are subtle differences, but it is precisely this period detail that is always so fascinating for a designer. In some ways it offers a bigger challenge to take on something so close in period to one you've designed before.

THE BEGINNING

I always work with John Bright at Cosprop and I start by pulling stock costumes from the racks that might feel right for a character. You'd imagine that after *Sense and Sensibility* and *Pride and Prejudice* there would be a huge stock, but most of those costumes seem to be out in exhibitions all over the country. My biggest challenge was trying to do this film on a quarter of the budget that I had for *Sense and Sensibility*.

In my mind was the thought that Highbury is a provincial town, so we should not be looking for the French-influenced high fashion of the kind you'd find in London. I wanted the day-to-day clothes of a small town and I found many of my ideas from the Hampshire County Museum.

Jenny shows Diarmuid fabrics at Cosprop.

OPPOSITE: *Mark Strong as Knightley.*

Emma and Harriet.

ABOVE: *Emma in her aubergine outfit.*
BELOW: *(left to right) Mrs Weston, Mrs Elton, Mr Elton.*

EMMA

It helps when casting is done well in time, as on this production, so that you are able to develop design ideas with the person in mind. When they cast Kate, I had her in for a fitting. Kate is tall and I knew that we were going to have to make virtually everything for her but I had already been tracking down authentic costumes from the period to use as the starting point. I had been looking for stylish clothes with clean lines, not heavily laced – unfussy things, but which showed she had money. She would have had a style which she knew suited her. I found one dress, which was made of a white butterfly muslin that looked terribly good on Kate. The cut of it was excellent and she looked lovely. It gave her bust the right look, it fell properly, it was elegant but very simple. So we used that as a pattern and I got fabrics together that I thought were the right colour range for the character of Emma.

COLOURS

People naturally fall into colour schemes and it becomes very clear what someone's colours are going to be. I imagined Emma going to Ford's shop in Highbury and the fabrics there that would have attracted her. Her colours became green-blues to grey-blues and the whites, of course, which were so popular at that time. She also had deep aubergine – a muslin with an aubergine-coloured print on it for example – and a dusty, maroon brown which appears both in a coat and a brown-striped dress. It evolved into quite a tight colour scheme, but they are rather unusual colours; the blue and the aubergine are quite distinctive.

For Mrs Weston, I went for a more autumny colour scheme and Mrs Elton came out quite green – from yellow into the blue-greens. I have given her an apricot-coloured dress too because I try not to be too slavishly rigid with the colour schemes.

HARRIET AND JANE

In the first fitting I did for Harriet Smith, I went too far and made her look like a girl from a charity school, instead of a paying boarder at Mrs Goddard's school. Of course, if she'd looked like a penniless orphan, Emma wouldn't have paid her any attention. So we moderated our ideas and gave all the school girls a sort of school uniform of muslin frocks, brown capes and bonnets. I wanted to reflect Harriet's growing confidence and the fact that she has been taken up by Emma. So gradually we see her wearing better clothes which we hope the audience will think are hand-me-downs from Emma.

Harriet Smith.

Jane Fairfax has to be elegant. She has been brought up as companion to Colonel Campbell's daughter and so would have had good clothes. He wouldn't take her into society without dressing her well. We felt she'd not have a huge wardrobe, but that it would be well-made and quite cosmopolitan. With Olivia Williams, I came to realize that 'less is more'. We trimmed one dress but, when she tried it on, we decided to remove all the trim. She stands well and has beautiful shoulders, so the simple well-cut clothes worked best. We chose more mature colours for her dresses – darker grey-greens and blues – because we felt she would have seen more of the realities of the world than Emma.

THE MEN

The mark of distinction in men's clothes of the period was the use of sharp tonal contrast between the jacket and breeches. Knightley does show some of that, because we need to see that he is a gentleman, in spite of his probable preference for more practical garments. But on the whole his clothes and waistcoats are similar in colour and he wears moleskin and country fabrics. Frank Churchill, on the other hand, always has completely contrasting lights and darks of colour in his costume.

Jane Fairfax.

Mark Strong on costume

'My overriding feeling about Knightley was he's a country gentleman, who runs his estate in a very practical way. He is comfortable with himself and his surroundings. At my first costume fitting, Jenny brought out wonderful fabrics – moleskin, velvets and felts – in dark greens, browns and mushroom colours; all very autumnal. It felt so right.

'I assumed this was the sort of thing everyone would be wearing. But then I arrived on set and saw Mr Elton in his stark black, and Frank Churchill in his flashy London clothes of contrasting maroon and cream, and I realized she'd pitched it all perfectly. The clothes helped me enormously; they felt so comfortable and never allowed me to slip into generalized "Regency acting"; you know, wandering around harrumphing in your high collar.'

LEFT: *Frank Churchill and Knightley.*

Jenny Beavan: 'The only reason I seem so calm is because I have the most fantastic team. I'm not soldiering on alone!'

ABOVE: *Alistair Petrie: 'The great thing about boots and breeches is that it doesn't matter whether or not you look like an extra from Emmerdale Farm, you feel as if Sean Connery is your ugly older brother.'*

LEFT TO RIGHT: *Stephen, Anna and Jenny adjust the costumes.*

Miss Bates and Mr Woodhouse.

THE OLDER GENERATION

We wanted to make a point that the older generation had not changed their style of dressing for many years – Mr Woodhouse because he hates change, and the Bateses because of lack of money.

Mrs Bates had been the wife of the vicar of Highbury but, as a widow with a small pension, had fallen on hard times. Even though she's poor, we felt she'd have kept some exquisite pieces of lace, and probably one good evening dress. Sylvia Barter has the most perfect face, so we framed it with lace and added gentle layers everywhere else.

Prunella Scales wanted Miss Bates to look really thin, as if she'd been undernourished in the latter part of her life and, though her linen may be very darned, it will always be well-washed. We gave her two very practical day frocks, a tea dress and an evening gown. We felt that her friends in Highbury would make sure she somehow had fabric for this.

Mr Woodhouse is notoriously afraid of draughts so I found some little shawls for him to wear. I even had one knitted. We thought he'd wear felt and velvet in warm, rich colours. Mary Hillman and I discussed what he might wear on his head. As a man of the Old School, he'd probably still favour an old-fashioned wig. At home, he might remove this and put it on a wig-stand by his chair. Being susceptible to the cold, we were sure he'd have a cap, so we ferreted out this squashed-looking velvety hat that moulded beautifully onto Bernard Hepton's head. Whenever he came to try on his costumes, he'd instantly drop his face into a 'poor Mr Woodhouse' expression, which really made his clothes work.

COSTUME FITTING FOR BERNARD HEPTON: *'Mr Woodhouse is my favourite character in all of Jane Austen,'* says Bernard. *'He is kind and generous, but he is also manipulative and selfish. He is "out of his time" and does not quite understand "modern" behaviour. Rather like me!'*

JENNY ON CHOOSING HATS

This is a marvellous period for hats. To be aware of this you just have to look at the women's monthly magazines in the Victoria and Albert Museum, or the costume reference books and paintings of the period. Hats were very popular and milliners had some very quirky ideas. John Bright has to take the credit for the hats in *Emma*.

When Kate arrived for her first fitting she said, 'Oh, I hate bonnets.' We tried on a few and she was right, they didn't make her look powerful enough. Bonnets seemed to suit the gentler characters, like little Harriet or Mrs Weston. But to give Emma her status as 'First Lady of Highbury' hats seemed more appropriate.

KATE ON HER HATS

I'm quite good on clothes. I've never done a bonnet-show but I knew I'd look terrible in them and I did. So we decided Emma would wear hats, which made a strong statement about her. They were stylish and made me feel powerful and, because they were quite big, people had to keep their distance. They occasionally caused trouble particularly when Samantha Morton and I had to get close together for a two-shot. She had this bonnet we called E.T. because it had such a huge brim. The hats were like lethal weapons; the slightest turn and we could knock each other's head off!

Wardrobe, Make-up and Kate check continuity with Sue Clegg.

Mrs Weston.

Emma at the Crown Inn Ball.

MAKE-UP AND HAIR DESIGNER:
Mary Hillman

My research for the film came from two main sources – Kenneth Garlick's book on Thomas Lawrence's paintings and the Regency portraits in the National Gallery. Jenny Beavan and I talked a great deal about the look for each character and I went to most of the costume fittings so that I could see how she was piecing together the costumes. I always start with an idea for each character but it usually evolves once you meet the actors.

THE WOMEN

Women's hairstyles for this period were usually very simple and neat. This suited me because in general I'm not in favour of using wigs, and given the speed with which we were shooting, it helps not to have to do a lot of re-dressing of wigs in the evening. We were lucky to be able to use most of the girls' natural hair, with various bits and pieces added.

For the make-up I wanted to go for a natural look, called a 'straight corrective'. One of the most difficult things was convincing the actresses that they looked good without a lot of eye make-up and lipstick. We tinted eyelashes and urged everyone to stay out of the sun. In those days, a tan on a lady was considered very coarse. As soon as anyone was cast we urged them to take care of their nails, so that they wouldn't be embarrassed to show their hands for piano playing or other close-up work.

Emma

For the character of Emma, I originally thought that I would have her hair quite simple. But it was very important to Kate that her hair had movement in it. She wanted a bit of a ponytail occasionally that made her look cheeky when she tossed her head. It gave her more pertness. Her natural hair was short so we decided to give her extensions rather than a wig. This would enable her to keep that lovely long look at the back of the neck, which you're in danger of losing with a wig. I was worried because the length of her real hair was only two inches at the back and I wasn't sure how to keep it up without showing pins. In the end I used a very strong setting solution and every time she wasn't in shot I put in pins. Poor Kate, every time she went out I was chasing after her.

Jane and Harriet

Both Jane Fairfax and Harriet Smith were straightforward. Olivia has a classic beauty so I decided to keep her look absolutely simple. Samantha as Harriet has to look perfectly natural as she wouldn't have

had anyone to dress her hair. She'd have just put her hair up in a simple bun, which was correct for the period. We cut the front of her hair so that we could add some soft curls around her face, and put a very subtle colour rinse through, to lighten it and make her look even younger.

Miss Bates

There was a lot of discussion about Miss Bates before we finally decided on her look. I originally saw her as a 45-year-old, but Diarmuid described her as a 'menopausal survivor' and Prunella agreed that she should be older. We chose not to grey her own hair, but to give her a wig. She had a lot more make-up on than the others because we decided to make her complexion very ruddy. And she felt that very few people of her age in that period would have had a full set of gleaming teeth, so each day we stained the edges of her front teeth brown.

THE MEN

I wanted the younger men to look as natural as possible by today's standards, but that's not easy with this period. Knightley would be very secure in his appearance; he'd have a good haircut, but probably wouldn't have bothered to have his hair tonged into position. Frank Churchill, on the other hand, being the young foppish character that he is, would have had very styled hair. Ray had naturally curly blonde hair, which was ideal, so all we had to do was add some length at the back.

Mr Woodhouse would have been at his peak some thirty years before and is a man who doesn't like change, so his look wouldn't be at all up-to-date. When I first spoke to Bernard he said the only thing he wanted was a pair of bushy sideburns, so I said 'What about a wig?' He went along with the idea. It was a hard front wig that was a throwback to another age. His great friend, Mr Perry, who is of the same generation as Mr Woodhouse, also wore a wig, as did the footmen because they were in livery.

ABOVE: *Olivia Williams as Jane (left) and Samantha Morton checks her make-up (right).*

Miss Bates gets the final make-up touches from Penny.

ABOVE: *Frank Churchill at the Crown Inn Ball.*

BELOW: *Mr Woodhouse in his wig.*

Kate can't resist the Marilyn Monroe wig on the make-up truck.

KATE BECKINSALE ON HER HAIR EXTENSIONS

Because my hair was shortish I was given the choice of wig or hair extensions. Wigs are just a nightmare, but I'd had hair extensions before and they're great. The trouble was that I had to wash them every night, and they were long, thick, and very heavy; I could hardly lift my head when they were wet. I don't usually wash my hair every night, and certainly not when I've come back late from filming and have about two minutes to eat supper, learn my lines for the next day and try to get some sleep before an early morning start. It became my drama of the afternoon to keep myself entertained: 'Maybe I won't wash it tonight, I'll wake up early and do it then.' Then I'd wake up and the gloom would hit me and I'd wish I'd done it the night before.

Also, I don't think they're made to have hot rollers in for two hours twice a day and by the end of filming some were coming loose. My lovely driver Brian, who didn't realize I had extensions in, found one in his car one day. He came to see me with it held in his fingers, looking very concerned. 'Are you all right?' he whispered. It had glue on the end and it looked like a piece of real hair that had been yanked out of my scalp. I explained that it wasn't real – I think he was worried that I had terrible alopecia!

BEAN BABY

Mark Strong remembers his most trying scene: 'Emma and Knightley have quarrelled and he stays away from her for some time. On his first visit to Hartfield after this, it is obvious that they are still tense with each other. Isabella and John Knightley are there with their five children. Andrew has written this wonderful scene: Knightley and his brother are playing a game, throwing the children into the air. Emma stands apart, holding the baby and she and Knightley keep exchanging glances, wondering if they can ever be friends again. Then Knightley crosses and takes the baby from her and, as Andrew puts it, "spreading his tenderness both girl and baby," says, "You and I shall never be enemies."

'I was really looking forward to this scene and arrived on set with this warm glow. We rehearsed with a shiny plastic doll until we were ready to shoot and then the real baby was handed to Kate. Diarmuid whispered, 'Action', I crossed the room and suddenly everything erupted into howling baby! We set up again. More howling. We tried everything: squeaky toys, lullabies, feeding, absolute silence in the room, lots of noise in the room. There were two babies, but only one lacey nightie and hat. So the substitute was brought in and the kit changed. Same thing. Every time they heard 'Action', they'd go from smiling to crying, on cue. The babies (and clothes) were swopped several times, but it was no use. In the end, we had to move on to another scene, deciding we'd try the following day, with younger babies. 'Feed them and they'll just sleep,' all the crew with children said knowingly.

'Three days and eight babies later, we still hadn't shot the scene, which only consists of six lines. I started to feel like a boxer going into the ring, trying to be all confidence, thinking: 'This is going to great. I can really do it this time,' but, at the back of my mind, was the fear that I'd be defeated again. The final baby was extraordinary; it cried by quacking like a very loud duck.'

For Kate, the size of the babies was the first shock: 'They were big bruisers, about the size of four-year-olds, really heavy, and then they wouldn't stop crying. You're holding it, praying it won't make a sound and you suddenly realize you're supposed to be acting this touching scene. The whole room was incredibly tense. When I handed the last one to Mark and it quacked in his face, we got hysterical. Diarmuid got cross, but it was impossible not to laugh.'

Time was running out. The order went out for a dummy baby to be made. Stephen Miles was given the job: 'When I was asked if I could instantly create "a-something" for a prop baby, I thought that what we needed was a baby-shaped bean-bag. It had to have the weight and floppy head-movement of a real baby. The Art department provided a large piece of calico and while I cut and sewed it into a baby-shape, Jonathan, the office runner, was sent post-haste to the local Co-op to buy the stuffing.'

'All I'd been told was to buy lots and lots of dried beans and bird seed,' says Jonathan, 'so I raced round filling the trolley to overflowing with every pack of each that I could find. At the checkout, the man asked, "Is it a new diet, sir?" Without thinking, I said, "It's to make a baby," and then blushed very red, as I saw his look.'

The beans were hastily sewn into the baby-shaped bag, it was dressed in the lace nightie and cap and rushed to the set.

'The quacking baby was my lowest point,' says Mark. 'After that, acting with Bean Baby was heaven.'

Kate and Baby Number One.

Stephen proudly shows off Bean Baby.

ABOVE: *Sam Bond, having children of her own, shows Mark how to hold Bean Baby.*

LEFT: *Running repairs.*

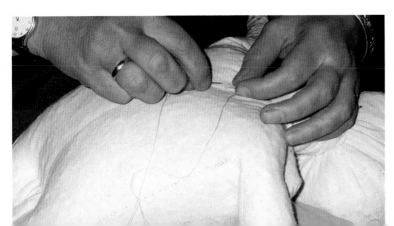

CHAPTER 5

The final scene

DURING the scripting process, a crucial discussion took place over one fundamental question: 'How do we end the film?' Screentime was tight, the novel's ending is extended, and many aspects of it felt too literary to work successfully as drama. Andrew Davies' solution was to invent a harvest supper, which would bring together all the loose plot lines and all the main characters.

The idea was enthusiastically received by the production team, who then had to face the challenges of realizing it on film. The following pages document some of the script-to-screen processes involved.

CONCEIVING THE IDEA:
Andrew Davies

The resolution of the plot is very lengthy in the book and, in parts, I don't think is all that brilliant. For example, getting Robert Martin and Harriet Smith together seems unnecessarily complicated – Emma sends Harriet to London, so you have to have Knightley sending Robert there on business, which I don't think he would have actually done. And in the book there are a number of little scenes after the engagement of Knightley and Emma which would take up a lot of screen time. So we would have gone from a big scene – the proposal – to a series of rather little scenes, a lot of which are off the spine of the story.

So I wondered if it wouldn't be possible to think of some kind of event, other than a wedding, which would bring all the characters together and tie up all the loose ends. I then imagined a kind of harvest supper, like in Hardy's or Tolstoy's novels – all that lovely stuff of bringing the harvest home and the haymakers and the good gentle-

'Harriet had always liked Robert Martin; and his continuing to love her had been irresistible' (Jane Austen).

OPPOSITE: *Knightley and Robert Martin in the harvest field.*

The scene is set for the harvest supper.

man farmer; a time when you need every man, woman and child in the community to work together. So I wrote in a scene where we see the harvesting in the fields and then a sequence of the harvest supper itself, where we show Knightley as an ideal old-fashioned landowner who wanted to share and celebrate with his tenants. I hoped this would form a nice contrast with the Eltons, who think it very eccentric of him to invite his tenants.

Though England didn't have a revolution, I think it must have been quite a narrow thing. The Georgians depended quite a lot on the Knightleys of this world, though few were probably as enlightened as he was. These landowners weren't decadent aristocrats who lived millions of miles away from their tenants and just withdrew the profits. They were actually there managing their estates. It's like old-fashioned conservatism really.

I wanted to do something in the screenplay that gave a sense of this wholeness in the community. I thought that Knightley would say a few words about his forthcoming marriage, but the speech would also be about stability and continuity. Perhaps Knightley has idealized it in this respect, but he shows that it is possible, and that he will be an example. So he's saying that he's going to be moving to live with Emma in her father's house, but that nothing else will change; that he'll continue to look after his tenants, which is an important thing. I think that in a historical period like the one we're living through there's a nostalgia – an 'angry' nostalgia even – for any time where you had some sense of fairness – where you might not have had much money but you could believe that you would be treated fairly.

DIRECTOR'S APPROACH:
Diarmuid Lawrence

Andrew wrote a scene that not only ties up all the loose ends of the plot, but also provides a romantic resolution to the film. But storytelling goes beyond the narrative of the text. The director contributes to the storytelling, as does the design, the music, the choreography, the lighting and so on. So my job is to deliver the full narrative and visual value of the scene onto the screen.

Putting together all the elements we had to consider for these two days was like assembling a giant jigsaw. With our puzzle there were many ways it could have been pieced together, but only two days could be allotted to this location. Which was the best way to tackle it?

In film terms, it's a long scene and the problems are compounded by its having every main character in it. In addition, dancers were involved as well as a band and dozens of supporting artists who appear as Knightley's tenants and servants. Even with extra help and the earliest possible start, the costume and make-up departments couldn't get them all onto the set for the start of the day. So I'd have to start shooting small sections of the scene using actors as they became available.

The scene should start in golden afternoon light as everyone arrives, slip into the steel blue of evening and end in candle-lit night. However, blacking out those enormous windows for night was a big job and, as we knew it would be quicker to take down the masking than put it up, we decided to pre-rig and shoot all the night scenes first. This would cause problems for other departments and for the actors who would have to play the resolution of the scene before they'd done the beginning.

During the course of the evening, we have to see a full banquet,

Diarmuid and Mark discuss Knightley's banquet speech.

Diarmuid checks the shot.

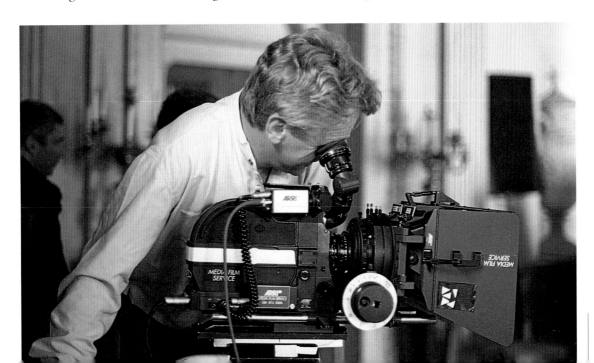

Remi and Diarmuid prepare to shoot the scene.

The musicians strike up for the dance even though the dancers won't be there until the following day.

again in three states: laid out for the start of the meal, half-way through the feast, and then being cleared away. I was also keen to have a whole pig roasting in the fireplace, which meant we needed a special effects team working alongside. The chimney was permanently blocked so the fumes had to be extracted through a complicated duct system, hidden under layers of autumn leaves.

The hall at Broughton Castle was beautiful, but it threw up some staging problems for me. Ideally, I had wanted a minstrels gallery at one end and the fireplace at the other. This would have enabled me to tuck the musicians away and only see them when we chose, as we could only afford them for one of the days. I would have put the top table at the gallery end with the two long tables running from it down either side of the room. This is because one of the most important moments in the scene is where Emma walks across to Harriet and Robert Martin. She wants to acknowledge how mistaken she's been about him by shaking his hand as an equal. To emphasize the change in her, to see how much she has grown up if you like, I wanted to make this gesture a very public one by having her walk the length of the room to reach him. Unfortunately, the fireplace here was on a side wall and so the tables had to be re-arranged to engineer this moment.

We had three dances to stage, two of them as background to important conversations. This necessitated everyone wearing hidden earpieces to relay the pre-recorded music. For the final dance I'd envisaged a crane shot, so the camera could lift away from the action. Cranes are expensive so, again, only one day was possible. Because the band and the crane couldn't fit into the room at the same time, each had to come on separate days, which meant the dances had to be done without the musicians. This wasn't a problem music-wise as it had been pre-recorded, but it means you will never see the musicians and dancers in the same shot!

We wanted the evening to feel enchanting without looking stagey. There should be a *Midsummer's Night Dream* feel to it, particularly in the final dance. This shows our three couples, who've been cast asunder, now happily with their partners, and backed up by a harmonious society. We then slightly pull the rug from under this idealized vision by cutting outside to see the chicken thieves at work again.

The nearest I came to losing my nerve was during the final dance. These period dances take up so much floor space, and we were battling with getting the crane to retract far enough for the wide shot at the end. With everybody lined up and ready and time running out, I just thought to myself, 'Please don't let me find I've got a camera operator with his head so squashed against the ceiling that we can't get the shot.' Thankfully, the crane could pull back just far enough – and no one forgot the dance!

SET DECORATION:
John Bush

The windows are decorated and the top table set for the start of the banquet.

Conceiving the idea was a challenge. It was the one place where the Art department did a sketch to work out roughly what we might do. In our general research for the film we found out that there were no special church decorations for weddings and so on, so we thought we should make the most out of the harvest supper. We found some very nice descriptions of these from various parts of the country. We found details not only of the meal but of things like the harvest home ceremony, where they would decorate the haycarts. There was a lovely account of somebody travelling around the country at that time coming across this procession of villagers who had created a queen of the harvest and decorated the haycart in quite an outrageous way. So we thought it would be nice to use all these elements in the harvest supper.

Broughton Castle was such a wonderful location for the scene. One of the great features of the room was these lovely windows which we decided to fill with decorations. In one of the research books there were several beautiful little vignettes of sheaves of corn with musical instruments and scythes in them. We thought we would take that as our inspiration for creating the windows, using those images of the harvest and the fruits to create lovely shapes and colour.

Val Biro's woodcut provides the inspiration for the set decoration.

RIGHT: *The harvest decorations are finished, ready for filming.*

BELOW: *John (left) helps Clive Brown to lay the tables.*

We found that there was an obvious layout for the tables: a top table for the gentry and side tables for the tenants. We decided to cover the top table with white damask, but we left the other tables as bare oak. We didn't want to get too overly pretty because everything was heightened by the beauty of the stone. There is a danger of it tipping over into interior design. We wanted it to look as if the villagers had done it using the materials and fruits of the harvest, but we also knew that they went to great lengths to decorate. So we tried to keep it within these boundaries.

We ordered a lot of slightly waxed, wine-coloured beech leaves and used them extensively. At the time I ordered them I wasn't sure where they would be used. But the colour worked so well that we decorated both the walls and the top table with them. The scene was a little out of the ordinary and we were given a very free hand, so we had great fun with it

THE BANQUET:
Debbie Brodie

Harvest chickens.

It was a common thing for a landowner to repay his tenants for the year's hard work by providing a harvest-home supper. Although the wealthy could eat to excess, the diet of the poor at this time was desperate. The people in the country fared better than town dwellers because they could poach and many of them were able to grow their own few vegetables or keep chickens. A party like this would provide one of the few occasions where they could eat plenty of meat.

When you are cooking for films, there's a fine line between being completely authentic and making the food work in front of the camera. I always go slightly over-the-top, otherwise things just look rather flat and brown. The food shouldn't be the focus of the scene; it's a background. But it does have to help the storytelling. It should say: 'wealth' and 'celebration' and 'autumn'.

I made bread in the shape of wheatsheaves, enormous ones to decorate the serving tables and windows and then 50 individual ones, so there could be one set at each place. I built huge pyramids of seasonal fruit, to give a richness of colour to the tables, and dozens of large open fruit tarts. We piled plates high with elaborate pies. Some of these were made so they could be eaten, but most were just filled with bread to save costs. And then, of course, there were the meats. We had ribs of beef, sides of hams and chickens by the dozen. These were roasted with their feet on to give a rural edge; people were less sentimental about animals then. Diarmuid wanted to have a whole pig roasting in the fireplace. I always try to avoid suckling pigs or boar's heads at banquets as they seem clichéd, but this was an enormous pig, so it looked right.

The scene was shot over two days and, when you use real food, it's difficult to keep everything looking and smelling fresh. The actors, who have to sit near to it, somethimes for hours, are usually very tolerant, but the food itself can be less controlled. The fruit tarts get particularly soggy, so I'd planned to replace them for the second day. Unfortunately, over night, the spare pastry cases had been thrown away by mistake, so I had to use every trick I knew to keep those tarts together.

'All is safely gathered in.'

On the camera recce, the team discovers that the chimney is blocked, and plans are drawn up to funnel the fumes through an air duct so that a whole pig can be roasted.

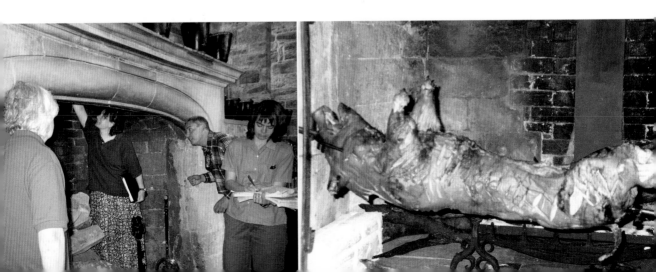

Debbie has ten minutes to carve the pig and crisp it with the blow torch.

The biggest challenge for me was the fact that the scene was shot out of order. We started at the end of the meal, then went to the middle, had a few shots of all the food being cleared away and then ended with the tables beautifully laid with all the food for the start of the banquet. This meant we had to have several copies of each piece of food. For continuity reasons – and for my own sanity – we decided to lay out the tables as if for the start of the meal. This is how it would have to look 36 hours later. We then started to take away food, to carve into the hams, crumble the bread, cut the pies and tarts.

Everyone's plate had to look used, some with leftovers on, and the wine glasses emptied. We had to have two pigs: one that we could carve into, the other to leave whole for the final shots. I hired my butcher and a mobile barbeque for the day to cook these, as they need constant supervision. There is very little time in between set-ups in which to change everything. I suddenly found I had less than ten minutes to carve the whole pig down to the bone and crisp it up, so it looked as if it had just come off the fire. This was precisely the time that Remi decided to black out the room. I think I should go into the record books for 'The quickest pig carving on the floor in the dark'!

Sound recordist Jim Greenhorn attaches a radio microphone to Dominic Rowan.

COSTUME:
Jenny Beavan

The ladies dance in their simple muslin frocks.

This scene was the biggest problem for me, as it was an invented scene. Jane Austen writes such acutely well-observed scenes and people that it's easy to design. You know what it'll look like. But when a scene is imposed in this way it is hard to imagine it costume-wise, and that's how I design, by imagining the whole scene.

I felt the harvest supper at that time would have been a thank you to the workers, provided and paid for by the landowner but not attended by him or the top people. He might show his face and propose a toast and, if it were Knightley, go round and chat. But this scene seemed to be half harvest supper and half engagement party, with both villagers and landowners. I didn't know how to pitch it. It wasn't a problem about what to make, each character already had a wardrobe of clothes to cover every sort of occasion, it was a case of what would look right.

We discussed it endlessly; we knew that the tenants would be in their best clothes but what about the top table? Rich people would always change for dinner, the ladies usually wearing silk. But how would this fit in with the roasting pig in the fireplace? The Art department was decorating the hall with the fruits of the harvest, which gave a rustic feel and seemed to suggest simple frocks. But could we justify this?

We asked ourselves: if rich people are entertaining the village and farm workers, would they dress *up* or *down*? We thought that Knightley would want to show respect for them but he could choose to do this either by dressing up to make them feel he was putting on the best show for them, or by dressing down to make them feel more comfortable and at home. We felt that Knightley, who doesn't normally go in for outward show, would prefer the latter.

The Eltons' comments about 'inviting the tenants', 'sitting down with hobbledehoys' and how they felt the whole thing was 'eccentric', made me realize that an occasion such as this wasn't normal. It gave us a licence to interpret the clothes more freely.

So we followed our instinct and put the ladies in simple white muslin frocks with hair decorations that echoed the set design. For these, we begged lavender and leaves from the Art deparment and threaded them on ribbons. We made an exception of Mrs Elton who, as usual, was overdressed in silk, lace, jewellery and an enormous hat.

When I saw it all come together on the set it looked right. Knightley has made an effort with the decorating and the food – to provide an occasion where his workers wouldn't feel uncomfortable and the simple clothes fitted in better with this.

Dancer Dee-Dee Wilde, a founder member of 'Pan's People', has her hem mended.

Once we'd made this decision, a couple of weeks ahead, everything else fell into place. The actual filming days were not then particularly difficult. Of course, we all had to start very early, because every character was needed on set at the beginning, but once they were ready there was only the maintenance work during the day and we had extra help. The only problem was the fact that the scene was filmed back-to-front. This didn't affect the main characters but it did cause difficulties with the cooks. Roasting a pig is hot, dirty work and the first thing we filmed was them removing it at the end of the meal. We only had one set of white aprons which would have to be clean for the start of the scene, to be shot later. We knew we couldn't actually make the aprons dirty – there wasn't time to wash them. So we used lots of water sprayed in patches. This made them look hot and dirty, but dried off leaving no stains, and we relied on the make-up department to make it work by dirtying hands and faces.

LIGHTING AND PHOTOGRAPHY:
Remi Adefarasin

Remi joins the kitchen maids.

Most films are shot out of order to some degree but this scene was shot back to front and sideways. I always push for a rehearsal of the whole scene before getting the camera out, so everyone knows what we're aiming for, but this scene was too complex for this to happen and we ended up pinching at bits and pieces. Economy was another reason for our deviation from good shooting practice. We could only afford dancers, musicians, steadicam and the camera crane for one or other of the two days.

My problems as director of photography became obvious on the pre-shoot recce when I looked up at the ceiling. It's a beautiful confection – like an upside down wedding cake – but we couldn't attach lights to it. We would only be there for two days, so we knew it would be far too costly to build and then disguise a scaffolding rig. Every corner of the room would be seen at some stage. The scene required three different lighting conditions: golden evening, then twilight, before going to candle-lit night. The costume and design work were sumptuous and I had to make sure they could be seen, and yet look natural.

Candle-lit night was the main lighting condition and was the most difficult to achieve. I like to light in a naturalistic way, capturing and enhancing reality. I hate phoney-looking lighting as it breaks the spell and destroys the illusion. Pure candle-light is quite difficult to capture, especially in large halls. Dozens of candles are needed to get an exposure and then it's so low that, when the actors move, they go out of focus. If you supplement it with electric light, it's very easy to swamp the candle-light. So my brief was to devise an authentic-looking lighting scheme that would allow us to shoot 360 degrees without touching the ceiling – or the budget.

During the recce, my brilliant gaffer, Jimmy Wilson, noticed some oak beams just beneath the ceiling. We asked Lord Seye's permission to put four screw eyes into the wood, one at each corner, and permission was granted. Jimmy used these to fix two lines of wire forming a cross. Large Chinese lanterns were then suspended from this wire. In the centre we hung a playlight – made by my wife converting a children's play tunnel by covering it with white parachute silk. When it's filled with bulbs, it gives out a magical glow.

Each leg of the cross could be dimmed individually so we could shoot in any direction instantly. This creation formed the shadowless glow for the hall. Soft cross-light was used to give shape and depth. For close work, I used white foam sheets to push extra light through. I often use pieces of window-net when lighting, and drape these over the sheets to fragment the light and make it non-electric. In this way, Sean, the camera operator, Jimmy and I tried to make Kate and Mark look even more beautiful than usual.

The Great Hall as seen on the camera recce with its 'wedding cake' ceiling.

ABOVE: *The outside lighting rig for golden evening light (top) and being blacked out for night (above).*

BELOW: *Remi and Jimmy discuss the lighting (left). Chinese lanterns and play tunnel (centre). Camera operator Sean Savage films the scene (right).*

The camera recce: is the room wide enough for the final dance?

THE DANCES AT DONWELL:
Jane Gibson

Jane Austen always uses dances dramatically. Important things happen at balls, and the story often moves on. Although the harvest supper scene was an invented one, I kept this very much in mind when I thought about the dancing. Story and dance should always be linked. Throughout the book and the film, we are kept guessing about who will end up with whom: will Harriet succeed with Knightley, or will he fall for Jane Fairfax's musical charms, and will Frank carry off Emma? It's all about match-making and mismatching, so I felt that the last image we see of them all should be one of harmony after disruption, with everything feeling it's in the right place. It was particularly important to see the three couples, each of which had been asunder, happily together, not only with each other but also as a group.

The occasion is a traditional harvest-time supper, a cross-class affair that only someone like Knightley could pull off with ease. The script indicates that, after all the loose ends of the plot are tied up, Knightley leads Emma down the length of the room (displaying his bride, if you like) until they reach the top. Then the rest of the assembled society falls in behind and dances harmoniously.

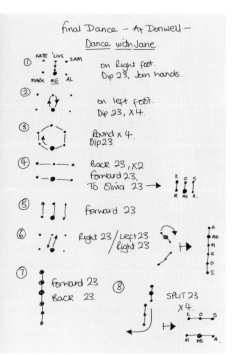

final Dance — At Donwell —
Dance with Jane.

① KATE 'LIVS • SAM
  • ↑ •
  MARK ME AL

on Right foot.
Dip 23, Join hands.

② • ✧ •
  • •

on left foot.
Dip 23, X4.

③ ⬡

Round x 4.
Dip23.

④ •—•—•
  •—•—•

Back 23, X2
Forward 23,
To Olivia 23 →

↑↑↑
M ME A.
K O S

⑤ ↑↑↑

forward 23

⑥ • ↑↑ •
  • ↑ •

Right 23/Left 23
     /Right 23

↻ ↦

A
ME
M
K
O
S

⑦ forward 23
   Back 23.

⑧ ↑↓ ↦

SPLIT 23
X 4.
K O S
M ME A.

LEFT: *Raymond Coulthard: 'Just before filming the final dance, Diarmuid caught me studying my dance diagram. He told me he'd once had to recreate the Battle of Trafalgar in a film, and a military historian he'd consulted drew up a very elaborate plan of how the battle was fought. He said it looked remarkably similar to my dance diagram! This made perfect sense to me. I was in six dances in* Emma *and each time it felt like going into battle.'*

We decided that after Knightley and Emma reach the top, Frank would lead Jane to the next position followed by Robert Martin and Harriet. Normally, the latter couple would go much further down the line because of their social rank, but we felt we could stretch a point at such an occasion and use it to display the three newly-engaged couples. They would then dance the first part, or measure, on their own, with everyone watching before expressing their approval by joining in.

We had already seen two country dances, the sort you would do on the village green. But now I wanted a stately dance, with some nobility. It had to be graceful, but sexy as this is our 'wedding scene'. No one single dance seemed to fit the bill so I ended up combining two. 'Mr Isaac's Maggot' is a very beautiful dance, but done in sets of two couples, so I lifted out the elements that worked for us, keeping the music, and added it to a much older dance called 'Step Stately'. The ensuing dance had the three men and three women in lines moving towards each other, then briefly holding the hands of their own partner as they turn, before they form a circle of six, an enduring symbol of harmony. They separate into lines of men and women again and move round each other until one line of six is formed facing the front. They advance and retreat, before the others add to the lines.

The step is not an easy one to do as it glides rather like an early waltz, but it was good to see it danced by masculine men and graceful women. The beautiful spatial patterns mirror the dynamics of the relationships. I felt it was all right to combine two dances as teachers at that time were always making up new ones. In fact, I think I might call it 'Miss Gibson's Stately Maggot'!

BELOW: *Dance rehearsal (left). Jack Murphy and Jane go through the steps with James Hazeldine (right).*

MAKE-UP:
Patricia Kirkman

I climbed aboard the make-up bus serenaded by the first tweetings of the dawn chorus as usual, and tried hard to remember where I had hurriedly packed everything the night before. Mary and Penny arrived moments later. To my dismay, my expensive shampoo had spilled during the move from the previous location and seeped into the carpet around my place, which was already soaking from the overflowing plumbing. Consequently, I was ankle deep in suds within minutes. A good start, I thought.

We had hired a large marquee and extra make-up artists to help us work miracles on the supporting artists, and so we had to untangle the spaghetti junction of electrical cabling for all the heated rollers, tongs, dryers and such like that they would be using to torture even the straightest of hair into the fashionable curls of the period.

Mary, Penny and I feel it is very important for us to look cheerful, enthusiastic and well-organized, so we have our own 'faces' on, however uncivilized the hour. We can then pour our energy into the actors, listen to their worries and with luck, deliver them on set content and ready to play their parts.

The make-up caravan – before the fray.

Patricia pins the back of Lucy Robinson's hair.

Mr Elton's over-dressed hair doesn't come naturally. Dominic Rowan suffers the indignity of Mary Hillman's heated rollers.

The first actors arrived bleary-eyed with scrubbed faces and very quickly our small bus filled up with a heap of coats, bags, scripts, breakfasts and a host of mobile phones. Dominic, the second assistant director, told them the phones wouldn't work on this location. How on Earth would everyone cope? He then discovered a place in the middle of a field where the phones did work and, within minutes, an orderly queue formed for this tiny patch of grass. Somehow we completed everyone's make-up and hair on time, sending them out with hair clips and nets on to preserve our creations through the windy walk to the Great Hall.

Word soon came back that the temperature on set was rising and the dancing hadn't even begun. We knew we were facing at least another ten hours of keeping each actor looking cool with every curl in place. Soon actors started turning up from set with black marks round their noses. We realized it was the residue from the log fire. This became so bad as the day wore on that I didn't know whether to offer them tissues or call a sweep.

Just before lunchtime the heavens opened, so I got out the bag of rain hats – undignified but essential. We quickly tied these onto all of our actors as they rushed desperately out into the cool fresh air for lunch.

We really had our work cut out during the afternoon as everyone was so hot and tired, and yet had to seem as fresh as when they had begun. At the end of the day they all came to have their make-up taken off as quickly as possible. We gave them each a glass of wine and as much sympathy as we could. My place looked as if a bomb had

The make-up caravan – after the fray.

gone off. I just had to sit down for two minutes before we set about cleaning and resetting all the hair-pieces, and preparing everything again for the next day's onslaught. My carpet was still covered in suds. At least I had clean shoes. How often people say that they too would like a 'glamorous' job. If only they knew the reality!

Cast and crew queue for lunch (above) and eat in the dining marquee (below).

The Lord and the Lady Seye and Sele

LOCATION OWNER:
The Lady Seye and Sele

The Great Hall has been used in many films over the years. It was wonderful for us to have something like *Emma* – a book we knew and which we thought would be done well. When we had *Joseph Andrews*, we just thought 'Help!' Before we knew it, we had skeletons all around the Great Hall and Michael Hordern's head in an iron contraption. The whole thing became very distasteful.

When I knew *Emma* was coming I dug out a copy of the book to re-read and raced through it in 48 hours. I looked in vain for the reference to the harvest supper. But when I thought about it, it seemed a very logical coming-together of all the different strands at the end of the novel.

It's always slightly tense at the beginning as we don't know who everyone is. But John Bush arrived and I instantly felt that here was someone who understood and cared about what he was doing.

They stripped out our furniture and this was a wonderful chance for me to clean the suits of armour which are usually perched up high. I don't remember when they last came down. I had a wonderful day rubbing away with wire wool and WD-40.

The most intriguing thing for me was the casting. When Mark Strong arrived in costume I just thought 'Oh that must be Knightley.' He seemed just right. The faces I had in my mind have actually worked out exactly. I didn't need to know which parts the actors were playing – I could guess.

Of course, a scene like this could be filmed in a studio but I always think that's like hearing a string quartet without the base line. A room like this gives a scene that strong underscoring.

OPPOSITE: *Emma and Jane make friends.*

RIGHT: *The three Susies – Clegg, Conklin and Birtwistle.*

MARK STRONG ON KNIGHTLEY'S SPEECH

Arriving on set and seeing this beautiful hall, decorated with the harvest fruits, brought home to me exactly the kind of man Knightley was. I was conscious that it was where Knightley comes from. Having seen him on everybody else's turf – say at Hartfield or at the Crown Inn – I was aware that this was now him at home. So the speech had to be Knightley 'on duty'. Whatever you'd seen of him before, you'd not seen this side of him: he's an employer, but an employer who cares and treats the people who work for him with respect. That's what I wanted to show and the setting certainly helped.

It was very bizarre having absolutely everyone in the cast sitting watching me. I didn't dare look at them. Every time I glanced down I could see rows of little gleaming faces all looking up at me expectantly. It was quite daunting having to do my speech in front of all the principal actors, the dancers, the extras, the band, the entire crew and several groups of tourists who'd actually come to see the embroidery exhibition at the castle!

The shot, which was done with the camera on a crane, started with Briar, his dog, eating a bone and then moved up to see Knightley. I remember thinking: 'I wonder if this is deliberate?' It seemed a good analogy: Knightley had proposed to Emma and been accepted and the dog's got his bone. It gave such a sense of satisfaction, which is exactly what Knightley should be feeling at that point.

BELOW: *Mark rehearses the speech (left). Diarmuid explains the shot (right).*

The screenplay

BY ANDREW DAVIES

1   FADE IN. EXTERIOR. HARTFIELD. *night*

A clear night in the country. Shadowy figures, three or four of them, running across the grass. There is some moonlight. We can see the silhouette of the house in the background, but the thieves are making for the chicken coops.

Crash! and splintering of wood as they break in the door. Now all the chickens are squawking and flying around – the chicken thieves grabbing them, trying to get at least two each, feathers flying everywhere.

Now they're off and running fast, back the way they came, chickens squawking under their arms – more chickens running across the grass … We hear a bucolic hoarse voice:

HEAD GARDENER: Ho! Ho there! Stop thief!

Bang! as he lets fly a shot. As the shot rings out, cut to:

2   INTERIOR. EMMA'S BEDROOM. *night*

Emma awakes with a start, and goes to the window in her nightie. Chickens are running around on the moonlit lawn, complaining loudly. And here's the cock, raising the alarm a bit too late. Close up on him as he rears his proud comb in the moonlight:

COCK: Cock-a-doodle-doo!

In on Emma's face.

3   EXTERIOR. HARTFIELD. *day*

Servant helping Mr Woodhouse into the carriage. Emma, already in, leans towards him to give him a hand …

MR WOODHOUSE: Thank you, my dear.

Miss Taylor is already in the carriage too, in her wedding gear. Emma arranges the rug over Mr Woodhouse's knees.

MR WOODHOUSE: Are you sure you are warm enough, Emma?

EMMA: Quite sure, father.

Now Mr Woodhouse looks across at Miss Taylor.

MR WOODHOUSE: There is still time to reconsider, my dear Miss Taylor. Come back home with us – James will not mind turning the carriage round and nobody you know would take it amiss.

Emma is amused and appalled in equal measure:

EMMA: Papa! Mr Weston would take it very much amiss!

MISS TAYLOR: Dear Mr Woodhouse – you are very kind. I shall miss Hartfield – but I am very happy to become Mr Weston's wife – truly I am.

She is too, brimming with it. Emma impulsively kisses her – a moment of emotion between them as Mr Woodhouse chunters on:

MR WOODHOUSE: But it's all very disturbing Emma. Six good hens and now Miss Taylor … it's a sad business – Ah, good morning, good morning …

Respectful villagers on the road are raising their hats. Emma acknowledges them graciously too, rather like royalty … When they've passed, the villagers [as you or I might] look at each other, as though to say 'All right for them'. The horses splatter through the mud.

Now they're going past a couple of ramshackle cottages of extraordinary squalor. A couple of ragged barefoot children have come out to gawp at them.

4	**INTERIOR. HIGHBURY CHURCH.** *day*

Miss Taylor [Mrs Weston as she will be] and Mr Weston standing before Mr Elton.

MR ELTON: … Repeat after me: I, William Francis Weston.

MR WESTON: I, William Francis Weston …

MR ELTON: Take thee, Anna Taylor.

MR WESTON: Take thee, Anna Taylor.

Mr Woodhouse wipes away a tear.

5	**EXTERIOR. HIGHBURY CHURCH.** *day*

Jolly wedding music as a radiantly happy Mr and Mrs Weston come out of church and get into their open carriage – everyone seems very pleased except Mr Woodhouse:

MR WOODHOUSE: Poor Miss Taylor!

EMMA: Oh, Father.

6   INTERIOR. HARTFIELD. DINING-ROOM. *night*

> *Emma and Mr Woodhouse dining alone, one at each end of the long polished table. Servants stand around. Miss Taylor's chair is still there in its place in the middle, though her place is not set. Mr Woodhouse speaks as though continuing his thought outside the church, which he is, really:*

MR WOODHOUSE: What a pity it is that Mr Weston ever thought of her!

EMMA: But Father, you wouldn't have Miss Taylor live with us for ever, when she could have a house of her own? And it's been a long time since I needed a governess.

7   INTERIOR. HARTFIELD. DRAWING-ROOM. *night*

> *A rather cosier scene, though the room seems far too big for two. Mr Woodhouse has his chair by the fire, and Emma is arranging the backgammon table. Mr Woodhouse is pursuing the same vein. [It's one of Emma's real virtues that she manages to be so patient with him.]*

MR WOODHOUSE: But she will never see us now. Randalls is such a distance.

EMMA: It's barely half a mile Father – depend upon it, we shall see Mrs Weston nearly every day.

MR WOODHOUSE: Well, I take it very ill when people get married and go away. I think they should not do it.

> *Emma sighs, but not ostentatiously.*

EMMA: Will you play at backgammon, Father?

> *We hear the bell ring: Mr Woodhouse starts.*

MR WOODHOUSE: Oh! Why will people call at such a late hour?

> *Emma cheers up. She has a good idea who it will be.*

8   INTERIOR. HARTFIELD. HALL. *night*

> *Knightley is giving his coat to the servant.*

KNIGHTLEY: There you are – and how are you Thomas, and your family?

THOMAS: Very well, Mr Knightley, thank you.

9   INTERIOR. HARTFIELD. DRAWING-ROOM. *night*

> *Knightley is vigorous, animated, decisive. [We are picking them up in mid-conversation.]*

KNIGHTLEY: Well, how did it go? I am sorry to have missed it. How did you all behave? Who cried most?

> *Emma smiles most of the time he's here. He cheers her up, she likes his sense of humour and his forceful manner. But apart from that, it's an odd sort of relationship. He's a bit like a much older brother, a bit like an uncle, a bit like a godfather, a bit of a father-figure.*

MR WOODHOUSE: Ah! Poor Miss Taylor!

KNIGHTLEY:	Poor Mr Woodhouse, poor Miss Woodhouse, if you like – but I can't say poor Miss Taylor! At the very least, she has only one to please now, not two!
EMMA:	Especially when one of those two is such a fanciful, troublesome creature? Is that what you were thinking?
KNIGHTLEY:	[*smiling*] Perhaps.
MR WOODHOUSE:	I'm afraid that's very true – I believe I am sometimes very fanciful and troublesome.
EMMA:	[*dashing to the rescue*] Dearest Papa! I didn't mean you! – Mr Knightley didn't mean you! I meant only myself. Mr Knightley loves to find fault with me you know –
MR WOODHOUSE:	Oh dear –
EMMA:	– in a joke – it is all a joke!
MR WOODHOUSE:	[*relieved*] Ah. Yes. Of course.

All that very fast. Now things have been put right. Emma can relax and smile at Knightley.

EMMA:	We always say what we like to one another.

And that's a line, and a look between them, that can carry lots of affection and trust.

EMMA:	Well, you want to hear about the wedding – we all behaved charmingly. Everybody punctual, everybody in their best looks, not a tear and hardly a long face to be seen.
MR WOODHOUSE:	Dear Emma bears everything so well.
KNIGHTLEY:	But every friend of Miss Taylor must be glad to see her married.
EMMA:	And you've forgotten one matter of joy to me – that I made the match myself!

Knightley shakes his head at her.

KNIGHTLEY:	You made a lucky guess, Emma, and that's all that can be said for you.
MR WOODHOUSE:	I wish you would not make matches, my dear, for whatever you say always comes to pass. Pray do not make any more of them Emma.
EMMA:	I promise you to make none for myself, Papa, but I must, indeed, for other people. Poor Mr Elton, now – I must look about for a wife for him.
KNIGHTLEY:	You'd do better to let the poor man alone, Emma.
EMMA:	But he has been here a whole year, and he's fitted out the vicarage so comfortably it would be a shame to have him single any longer!

10   INTERIOR. CHURCH. *day*

Sheaves of corn, etc. Mr Elton is a handsome young man, leading his congregation in vigorous hymn singing.

MR ELTON AND THE CONGREGATION:	All people that on Earth do dwell, Sing to the Lord with cheerful voice.

Him serve with fear, his praise forthtell,
Come ye before him and rejoice.

The Lord ye know is God indeed,
Without our aid he did us make.
We are his folk, he doth us feed,
And for his sheep he doth us take.

Emma's sharp intelligent gaze wanders round, and settles on Harriet Smith, sitting in a convenient shaft of sunlight like a young angel, with Mrs Goddard and the great girls and small girls from Mrs Goddard's school. Harriet is singing very fervently, she has a beautiful innocent face. Mrs Goddard feels Emma's look – she turns and smiles.

11   **EXTERIOR. CHURCH.** *day*

Mr Elton is shaking hands with people as they go out. It is Harriet's turn and she is accompanied by the small girls in her charge. Emma and Mrs Goddard walk through the churchyard on a higher pathway overlooking the scene below.

MRS GODDARD: Harriet Smith? She is somebody's natural daughter you know.

EMMA: She seems a very sweet genteel girl.

MRS GODDARD: Indeed she is. She is just now returned to the school as parlour boarder. She spent the summer at her friend's house in the country.

Harriet has moved to greet the Martin family. Miss Martin and Harriet kiss like sisters. Robert Martin, a young farmer, is all attention to Harriet. Emma's raised eyebrow makes Mrs Goddard say:

MRS GODDARD: It would be good for her to have the benefit of more varied society.

EMMA: Would you like to bring her on Tuesday to my father's whist party?

MRS GODDARD: Oh, Miss Woodhouse that is very kind!

EMMA: I should be glad to know her better.

12   **EXTERIOR. HARTFIELD.** *day*

Mrs Goddard and Harriet outside the front door. Harriet looks very nervous. Mrs Goddard rings the bell. Harriet clears her throat.

13   **INTERIOR. HARTFIELD.** *day*

People are grouped around small tea tables. Mrs Goddard, Mrs Bates, Miss Bates, Mr Elton, Mr Perry, Harriet, besides Mr Woodhouse and Emma – and a servant or two.

MR WOODHOUSE: Mrs Bates, let me propose your venturing on one of these eggs. An egg boiled very soft you know is not unwholesome – Mr Perry is not altogether against eggs, are you, Mr Perry?

Mr Perry is in conversation with Mrs Goddard.

MR PERRY: Three drops nightly in a glass of lemon juice – Against eggs? No, indeed – a soft-boiled egg will do you no harm.

MR WOODHOUSE: There now Mrs Bates – Mr Perry says it is all right – I think she does not hear, Miss Bates –

Mrs Bates is dying to get stuck into her egg, but it keeps coming closer and going back – now Miss Bates seems about to help her to it, but she gets sidetracked.

MISS BATES: Indeed she dearly loves a fresh egg softly boiled [*turning away, with the egg, to Mrs Goddard*] – Mr Knightley was so good as to let us have three dozen of his very best fresh laid eggs, and when his man William Larkins brought them round he said that Mr Knightley has left himself without an egg – imagine – no eggs at Donwell Abbey – but then he is so very generous –

Mr Woodhouse speaks across this, in counterpoint, to Mrs Bates, who is watching her egg ebb away from her on the tide, as it were.

MR WOODHOUSE: Serle understands boiling an egg better than anybody. I would not recommend an egg boiled by anybody else – but you need not be afraid – they are very small, you see – one of our small eggs will not hurt you.

MR ELTON: [*handing peeled egg*] Allow me to help you, Mrs Bates.

Up at the far end, Emma 'drawing out' Harriet:

HARRIET: And they have eight cows, two of them Alderneys – and [*she smiles fondly*] one a little Welsh cow, a very pretty little Welsh cow – and Mrs Martin said as I was so fond of it, it should be called my cow! Do you know the Martins, Miss Woodhouse? – Mr Martin knows you by sight very well – his farm is very near to Donwell.

EMMA: Then they must be Mr Knightley's tenants. I may have seen Mr Martin fifty times, without having any idea of his name – a young farmer is not at all the sort of person who would raise my curiosity.

HARRIET: [*rather dashed*] No, I suppose not. [*but rallying almost instantly*] But they have two parlours, two very good parlours.

EMMA: Indeed!

Emma is keeping an eye on Mr Elton, who is keeping an eye on her, while getting Brownie points for being nice to the old ladies. If Emma is to steer Harriet clear of the yeomanry, she had better get cracking on it.

EMMA: Well, Harriet, I'm sure these Martins must feel very proud to entertain a gentleman's daughter –

HARRIET: [*eyes down*] I do not know that my father is a gentleman, Miss Woodhouse.

EMMA: I am quite sure he is – but even so, and particularly bearing in mind the misfortune of your birth – you should be very careful who you choose as your friends.

Clearly we need a setting in which Emma can say this confidentially, without fear of being overheard. Mr Elton looks over, his eye naturally drawn to two good-looking girls with their heads close together.

HARRIET: Oh, do you think so?

Emma meeting Mr Elton's smiling gaze:

EMMA: I am quite sure of it.

MR WOODHOUSE: Miss Smith, what do you say to a little bit of apple tart? A very little bit? Let Emma help you to a very little bit of apple tart.

Mr Elton springs up, all gallantry.

MR ELTON: No, no, no – allow me.

He neatly serves a slice of tart on to a plate, and takes it over to Harriet, presenting it with a flourish. She takes it with a shy smile.

HARRIET: Thank you, Mr Elton.

Emma's face – delighted that he's paid Harriet this attention. Mr Elton beams ... and in Emma's imagination:

14   EXTERIOR. CHURCH. *day.* [*Emma's fantasy*]

Mr Elton and Harriet, arm in arm, just after their wedding. All the girls from Mrs Goddard's school are throwing apple blossom in a very sugary soft-focus scene. Mendelssohn, everything. [Mr Elton turns to camera:]

MR ELTON: How can I ever thank you enough, Miss Woodhouse, for showing me where true joy was to be found! Mrs Elton and I are eternally indebted to you!

HARRIET: And to think that I should turn out to be the daughter of a baronet!

15   **INTERIOR. EMMA'S BEDROOM.** *night*

> *Emma, at the window, dark outside, the room partly reflected in the glass, laughs at the way her fantasy has run away with her. But then:*

EMMA: [*aloud*] But why not? Stranger things have happened.

16   **EXTERIOR. ROAD.** *day*

> *Emma is walking out with Harriet, laying down the law:*

HARRIET: I do so wonder that you should not be married, so charming as you are!

EMMA: I must find other people charming – one person at least. I have very little intention of ever marrying at all.

HARRIET: Dear me!

EMMA: Why should I? I lack neither fortune nor consequence. If I were to fall in love, it would be different – but I have never been in love – it is not my way, or my nature.

HARRIET: But then to be an old maid at last, like Miss Bates!

EMMA: If I thought I should ever be like Miss Bates, I would marry tomorrow.

> *Robert Martin is coming the other way. Harriet has already seen him, and hasn't been listening:*

HARRIET: Oh, Miss Woodhouse – there is Mr Martin!

EMMA: Oh, really.

> *Harriet is very excited to see him. He raises his hat very respectfully to Emma, and she nods graciously, then he turns to Harriet with an eager smile.*

ROBERT MARTIN: I never thought to meet you walking here, Miss Smith!

Emma without looking too grand about it, begins to walk on slowly, and Harriet panics a bit.

HARRIET: Oh – dear – perhaps I should – excuse me –

EMMA: No, no, please – I shall wait for you, Harriet.

And she goes on a few yards, 'not sorry to have such an opportunity of survey'. Harriet's conversation with Robert Martin is very brief, but the body language is enthusiastic on both sides – Robert Martin is only awkward in that he behaves like a man who's suddenly bumped into a girl he's barmy about, without having a chance to get a few remarks together. Harriet is very animated when she runs to catch Emma up – and she turns to see if he'll turn – and he does.

HARRIET: Only think of our happening to meet him! Oh, Miss Woodhouse, please say what you think of him – do you think him so very plain?

Harriet clearly think he looks very nice – she does not expect the brutal answer she gets:

EMMA: He is very plain, undoubtedly – but that's nothing, compared with his entire lack of gentility. I did not expect much, but I had no idea that he could be so very clownish, so totally without air.

HARRIET: To be sure – he is not so genteel as – real gentlemen.

EMMA: Indeed, no! Consider Mr Knightley! Consider Mr Elton!

HARRIET: [*sadly*] Certainly he is not like Mr Knightley. But Mr Knightley is so very fine a man!

EMMA: And Mr Elton, who has paid you such particular attentions? You must see the difference.

HARRIET: Yes, I suppose there is a great difference.

EMMA: And I think Mr Elton is becoming very fond of you. [*Emma gets an idea.*] Harriet, have you ever had your likeness taken?

Long shot of the girls. Then we see it is Knightley's point of view, as he strides across the fields towards Randalls, carrying a brace of pheasants. 'Hmm,' he thinks.

16a   INTERIOR. RANDALLS. *day*

KNIGHTLEY: I don't know what your opinion may be, Mrs Weston, but I think this great intimacy between Emma and Harriet Smith is a bad thing.

A servant comes in and bobs a curtsey and Knightley hands her the pheasants and she turns and trots off.

MRS WESTON: Hang them straight away mind, Jane. Thank you, Mr Knightley. And why should you think it such a bad thing?

KNIGHTLEY: She is the very worst sort of companion that Emma could have.

MRS WESTON: You surprise me. Emma must do Harriet good, and Harriet is a sweet girl – surely her friendship will be good for Emma?

KNIGHTLEY: I think not. If you could not correct her, I hardly think Miss Smith will.

MRS WESTON: [*laughing*] I should be sorry if I had to depend on your opinion of my ability as a governess.

KNIGHTLEY: Hartfield will only put Harriet out of countenance with the other places she belongs to. How can Emma imagine she has anything to learn herself, while Harriet is presenting such a delightful inferiority?

17   INTERIOR. HARTFIELD. STUDIO. *day*

This is a room that Emma has had done up as a studio, in some previous enthusiasm for art. She has a proper easel and her previous efforts are tacked on to the wall, one or two framed – some in portfolios. Harriet is posed by the window with the light falling on her prettily. Emma is trying to draw Mr Elton's attention to the sitter rather than the portrait.

EMMA: [*softly*] Don't you think she makes a charming picture?

MR ELTON: [*gallantly*] Oh, yes, indeed! You have given Miss Smith all that she required. She was a beautiful creature when she came to you – but you have made her graceful and easy.

EMMA: No, no – she only wanted drawing out ... Oh – I shall never do justice to her. Do you see, Mr Elton? Her features are so delicate – and yet there's a peculiarity in the shape of the eyes, and the lines about the mouth ...

MR ELTON: Exactly – and that's just what you've caught – there she is, to the very life!

EMMA: Mr Elton, I've scarcely begun.

But Mr Elton has wandered off to admire her other work when he should be admiring Harriet.

MR ELTON:	But these are excellent!
EMMA:	No, no, nothing like – you will see when they come – my sister Isabella and her children – they would never keep still – her husband Mr John Knightley – he is not so bad, but Isabella said it didn't do him justice – so I resolved to give up portraits for ever – at least where there are husbands and wives in the case.
MR ELTON:	Ah, yes. But there are no husbands and wives in this case! Or should I say – not at present!

Emma smiles at Harriet. This is looking very promising, she thinks.

18   INTERIOR. HARTFIELD. HALL. *evening*

The finished portrait displayed on the easel. Knightley, Mrs Weston, Mr Woodhouse and Mr Elton.

MR ELTON:	Perfection! Absolute perfection!
MRS WESTON:	Miss Smith has not those eyebrows, I think.
MR ELTON:	Oh, no, I cannot agree with you!
KNIGHTLEY:	You have made her too tall.
MR ELTON:	Oh, no! Certainly not too tall – Consider she is sitting down! And the proportions you know must be preserved.
MR WOODHOUSE:	It is very pretty – but my dear, she seems to be sitting out of doors, with only a little shawl over her shoulders – and it makes one think she must catch cold.
EMMA:	But Papa, it's supposed to be summer, a warm day in summer. Look at the tree!
MR ELTON:	I regard it as a most happy thought, the placing of Miss Smith out of doors – and the tree, the tree is touched with such – inimitable spirit!

Here Knightley might catch Emma's eye – they both think Mr Elton is protesting too much.

MR ELTON:	Miss Woodhouse – might I appeal for the commission of getting the picture framed? If you would trust me with it, I could ride to London at any time! No, no! I will be bold, and insist that you entrust it to no one but me.

19   EXTERIOR. HARTFIELD. *day. [the next morning]*

Emma stands at the gate, as Mr Elton rides off into the distance, brandishing his precious drawing neatly rolled up in brown paper. Emma smiles. She's amused, but also pleased he's such a romantic lover for Harriet. As she turns to go in, Harriet hurries up from the other direction.

HARRIET:	Oh, Miss Woodhouse – you will never guess! He has proposed!
EMMA:	Already? But – are you quite sure?
HARRIET:	Yes – he says so quite clearly in this letter! Oh, Miss Woodhouse, what am I to do?

She gives Emma the letter.

EMMA: But this letter is from Mr Robert Martin.

HARRIET: Yes, didn't I say that? Do you think it's a good letter? Is it too short?

EMMA: [*thoughtfully*] It is a good letter – a very good letter – much better than I should have expected.

HARRIET: So – how should I reply? Oh, Miss Woodhouse – please advise me.

EMMA: Oh, no! The letter had much better be all your own. But your meaning must be quite clear – no doubts or demurs. You need not elaborate on your sorrow at his disappointment.

               She hands the letter back to Harriet.

HARRIET: [*looking down*] You think I ought to refuse him, then.

EMMA: Harriet! Are you in any doubt?

HARRIET: I ... had no notion he liked me so very much.

               She looks down at the letter – the thing is, she did have very tender feelings for Robert Martin before Emma started slagging him off, and the letter has revived those feelings. A little pause. We need to be aware of the enormity of what Emma is doing:

EMMA: [*carefully*] I lay it down as a general rule, Harriet, that if a woman doubts, she certainly ought to refuse him – but do not imagine that I want to influence you.

HARRIET: Oh! No, I'm sure – but if you would just advise me what I had best do – no, no, I don't mean that – as you say, one's mind ought to be quite made up ... Do you think I had better say no?

EMMA: Harriet, you must be the best judge of your own happiness. Do you truly prefer Mr Martin to every other man you have ever met? Harriet, Harriet, don't deceive yourself. Don't be run away with by gratitude and compassion.

Harriet wrestles with conflicting emotions for a few moments, then:

HARRIET: Miss Woodhouse – as you won't give me your opinion – I think – yes I have now quite determined, and have almost made up my mind – to refuse Mr Martin. [*piteously*] Do you think I am right?

If they have been walking, they should be nearing the door of Hartfield by the end of this next speech.

EMMA: Perfectly, perfectly right! Dearest Harriet! And now I can say what I could not say before, because I would not influence you – had you accepted him, I would have lost my friend. I could not have visited Mrs Robert Martin of Abbey-Mill Farm. Now I am secure of you for ever!

She ushers Harriet into the house. Harriet is smiling, but her eyes are full of tears.

20   INTERIOR. HARTFIELD. DRAWING-ROOM. *day*

In on Knightley's face. He is angry and incredulous. Emma is alarmed, almost frightened, but determined not to show it.

KNIGHTLEY: She refused him? Harriet Smith refused Robert Martin?

EMMA: Yes.

KNIGHTLEY: Then she's a greater simpleton than I thought. What is the foolish girl about?

EMMA: Oh, to be sure. A man always imagines a woman to be ready for anyone who asks her.

KNIGHTLEY: Nonsense. A man does not imagine any such thing. I hope you are mistaken.

EMMA: I saw her answer. Nothing could be clearer.

KNIGHTLEY: You saw her answer? You wrote her answer. Emma, this is your doing. You persuaded her to refuse him.

EMMA: And if I did, I should not feel that I have done wrong. Mr Martin is a very respectable young man, I am sure – but he is not Harriet's equal.

KNIGHTLEY: No, he is not. He is her superior in both sense and situation. Harriet Smith is the natural daughter of nobody knows whom – a girl with no connections – a parlour-boarder at a common school. She has been taught nothing that is useful. She is pretty and she is good tempered and that is all. My only scruple in recommending the match to Robert Martin –

EMMA: You recommended it?

KNIGHTLEY: Yes, I did – my only scruple was on his account – I felt he could have done much better, both as to fortune, and as to securing a useful helpmate – but I could not reason so to a man so much in love. And depend upon it, he had encouragement from her.

EMMA: She may have – been inclined towards him at one time, but the case is altered now. She knows now what gentlemen are; and no one but a gentleman has any chance with Harriet.

KNIGHTLEY: Nonsense, arrant nonsense!

A thought suddenly strikes Knightley.

KNIGHTLEY: You're not thinking of Elton, are you?

She is, but she won't admit it. She turns away, rather mortified.

KNIGHTLEY: If you are, depend upon it, Elton won't do. He may talk sentimentally, but he will act rationally. He knows the value of a good income. Harriet Smith has no chance there.

EMMA: [*laughing nervously*] I have no intention of marrying Harriet to anybody!

KNIGHTLEY: You have done your friend no favours, Emma. You have spoilt her best chance of happiness. It was badly done, and I am sorry for it. Good day to you.

And he goes out on that. Emma's face. She has been upset, but she won't surrender, because she knows better than anyone.

EMMA: You are wrong, Mr Knightley, and you will see you're wrong. And then you will be sorry.

End of Part One

21   INTERIOR. HARTFIELD. *day*

The drawing-room is full of people. Isabella, soft, docile, motherly, a fusspot. John Knightley, her husband, sardonic, quick-witted, quick-tempered too, but very fond of his wife and children and his home comforts. Their five children: Henry, John, Fanny, George and little Emma, the baby, who is in big Emma's arms.

Three nursery maids stand beaming – they are helping with the game. All the children except the baby are very excited; the game is rushing in turn at Knightley, who seizes them with a horrible growl and throws them in the air.

Start as Henry [the eldest] is being tossed up:

KNIGHTLEY: Huzzah!

Knightley gently lowers Henry and lets him slither to the floor. His eyes meet Emma's across the room – they are still a bit 'off' with each other after their quarrel. Both of them look away.

ISABELLA: I beg you would not toss them so high – John!

His sons are jumping up at him with excitement.

JOHN KNIGHTLEY: Nonsense, higher the better. Come, Fanny. Run to your uncle, fast as you can. Fee fi fo fum ...

The nursemaid steadies Fanny.

KNIGHTLEY:	Huzzah!
	As little Fanny rushes towards him to be grabbed and tossed up, she squeals with laughter. Mr Woodhouse gasps again, and turns to Isabella.
ISABELLA:	John, Papa is distressed!
JOHN KNIGHTLEY:	Well, well, that'll do then – no, no –
	[For they are jumping around begging for 'More, Papa, Papa!' ... 'More, Uncle George!'*]*
JOHN KNIGHTLEY:	Take 'em away, Betty; off with them, Jane ...
	The nursemaids bustle them off. Is there time for them to do little bows and say, 'Goodnight Grandfather'*? Into this:*
EMMA:	But my little Emma shall stay awhile.
JOHN KNIGHTLEY:	Aye, she makes no noise. You look well thus, Emma.
	Knightley, looking across, thinks so too. Quite a little moment: Emma as she would look as a beautiful young mother. She feels pleased and shy and a bit embarrassed for once. Knightley's heart melts towards her. He walks across the room to her.
	He holds out his hands for the baby, spreading his tenderness generously over both girl and baby, as it were. He takes the baby from her so naturally. Emma is looking at him rather anxiously because they parted in anger – and he looks back at her seriously.
KNIGHTLEY:	I remember holding you thus, once upon a time.
EMMA:	[*softly*] You and I must not be enemies.

KNIGHTLEY: No, you may do wrong, Emma, and I may be angry with you, but you and I shall never be enemies.

It's a very intimate exchange, there's more that's unspoken than spoken. They care about each other's opinions more than anything. Now Emma smiles with relief and the arrogance comes bouncing back.

EMMA: You forget that I've not been proved wrong. But I do hope Mr Martin is not very disappointed.

KNIGHTLEY: A man couldn't be more so.

EMMA: Then indeed I am very sorry.

They are back to being serious again. Then, Mr Woodhouse, who has been quietly chuntering away with Isabella all this time, erupts in a mild but quite querulous outburst:

MR WOODHOUSE: No, Isabella, there is no avoiding it, Mr and Mrs Weston have invited me, and we shall go, Christmas Eve or not, and whatever the weather! She is a bride and the visit must be paid I do believe – whatever the consequences!

Everyone else has fallen silent at this amazing, daring outburst. Mr Woodhouse has amazed everyone, including himself.

22 **EXTERIOR/INTERIOR. CARRIAGES. HARTFIELD.** *night*

Two carriages prepared for setting off in the snow. Mr Woodhouse being handed up into the first carriage, wrapped in sheepskins. John Knightley gets in the second one.

JOHN KNIGHTLEY: Aye, Mr Weston must have a very good opinion of himself, asking people to leave their own fireside in the depths of winter just for the sake of coming to see him. He must think himself a most agreeable fellow!

23   INTERIOR. MR WOODHOUSE'S CARRIAGE. *night*

Mr Woodhouse and Isabella. Both very well wrapped up and looking frightened but determined to survive this half-hour journey up the road. I think it would be nice if they were clasping hands.

MR WOODHOUSE: Go slowly James; go carefully!

24   INTERIOR. JOHN KNIGHTLEY'S CARRIAGE. *night*

John Knightley and Emma. He speaks with such savage intensity, that Emma is hard put to it not to laugh aloud.

JOHN KNIGHTLEY: And here we are, setting forward to spend five dull hours in another man's house – going in dismal weather, to return probably in worse – actually snowing at this moment, and more to come! Four horses and four servants taken out for nothing but to convey four idle, shivering creatures into colder rooms and worse company than they might have had at home.

EMMA: But you must know we are sure of excellent fires and everything in the greatest comfort.

The carriage is nearly at Mr Elton's house; he is standing outside looking very eagerly.

JOHN KNIGHTLEY: Here's the parson. He looks keen enough.

24a   EXTERIOR. CARRIAGE. PARSONAGE. *night*

One of the servants lets the step down on John Knightley's carriage – we see Mr Elton's ecstatic face before he climbs in next to Emma.

MR ELTON: My dear sir! Words cannot express my gratitude – on such a night as this – a Christmas party! Nothing could be pleasanter! Miss Woodhouse – this is an honour, nay, a delight!

JOHN KNIGHTLEY: Well get yourself in, man, and get the door shut, and the less said the better.

25   EXTERIOR. RANDALLS. *night*

A handsome double-fronted house in its own grounds, but a good deal smaller than Hartfield. Plenty of lights at all the windows, as the carriage arrives at the front door.

JOHN KNIGHTLEY: [*voice-over*] My first enjoyment will be to find myself safe at Hartfield again.

26   INTERIOR. RANDALLS. *night*

At the dinner table. Mr Weston, a good looking, very outgoing jolly type in his late forties, Mrs Weston, Mr Woodhouse, Emma, Isabella, John Knightley, Knightley and Mr Elton.

MR WESTON: A very happy gathering indeed! We want only two more to be just the right number – [*to Emma*] your pretty little friend Miss Smith – a bad sore throat –

MR WOODHOUSE: Oh, dear! Has Perry been called?

EMMA: Yes, and recommends she stay in bed –

MR WESTON: What a shame for her, and a sad loss for us –

EMMA: [*significant look at Mr Elton*] Yes, indeed –

MR WESTON: – and my son Frank! I had thought Frank would be here for Christmas – but it was not to be!

EMMA: I begin to fear that I shall never meet the famous Mr Frank Churchill.

MR WESTON: No, you are wrong, for he has promised to be with us in two weeks time! [*seeing Mr Elton puzzled*] Frank is the son of my first marriage Mr Elton – his poor mother died when he was but two years old – and her family undertook his care and education – and in gratitude he took their name.

JOHN KNIGHTLEY: [*sotto voce to Isabella*] Good deal of money in it I dare say.

MR ELTON: What age is the young man now?

MR WESTON: He is three and twenty – and though I say it myself, as fine a young man as anyone could wish to see – my only complaint is that Mrs Churchill likes to keep him at her beck and call in Yorkshire, so that he is not able to be here as often as he would wish.

MRS WESTON: Indeed – for I have never yet set eyes on him.

KNIGHTLEY: He should have come before this. To speak bluntly, it is his plain duty to his father, and to you, ma'am.

MRS WESTON: Well, I forgive him – it is a delicate business – Mrs Churchill rules at Enscombe, and she is a very odd-tempered woman, and his coming now depends upon her being willing to spare him.

ISABELLA: Oh, Mrs Churchill, everybody knows of Mrs Churchill – I feel sorry for that poor young man, to be constantly living with an ill-tempered person must be dreadful!

Isabella is very nice, though not very bright. She does live with a quick-tempered person, but she doesn't think of him like that, and without thinking touches his hand affectionately as she speaks.

Emma smiles, and Mr Woodhouse says:

MR WOODHOUSE: Yes, indeed, my love.

2 7   INTERIOR. RANDALLS. DRAWING-ROOM. *night*

Emma, with Mr Elton in close attendance, is looking at a miniature of Frank Churchill on the wall. Good looking and smiley. Mr and Mrs Weston on the other side of the room – Knightley closer.

MR WESTON: That is the young man in question. Frank to the very life!

EMMA: Then he is very handsome, is he not, Mr Elton?

MR ELTON: [*miffed*] I hardly know. [*he moves away*] Appearances may often deceive.

Mr Elton moves to speak to Mr Woodhouse, which leaves Emma and Knightley alone.

EMMA: As is well known, I intend never to marry – but I confess if I were to change my mind I have always thought that Mr Frank Churchill might be the man, for by all accounts he seems to be the very epitome of manly excellence!

Emma is speaking playfully, for general consumption – she has no idea she is wounding the sensibility of both Mr Elton and Knightley. Now Knightley speaks with some force and feeling – but it's just for Emma – he doesn't want to offend Mr Weston.

KNIGHTLEY: Apart from his disinclination to exert himself and do what he knows to be right.

EMMA: Mr Knightley, isn't it very unfair to judge a person's conduct when we don't know his situation? He may be unable to do what he truly wishes.

In the background, Mr Elton is taking another glass of wine to ease his discontent and raise his spirits, looking longingly across at Emma.

KNIGHTLEY: There is one thing a man can always do, if he chooses, and that is his duty. If he truly willed it, he could be here tomorrow.

There seems to be an excess of feeling in Knightley's words, which Emma spots:

EMMA: You seem determined to think ill of him.

KNIGHTLEY: Me! – not at all. He is a person I never think of from one month's end to another.

Knightley's feelings have been ruffled, and he turns away [we go with him]. Perhaps Emma could be talking happily to Mr Weston who is praising his son, and Knightley moves to Mrs Weston, who is looking at Emma.

MRS WESTON: How well she looks tonight.

KNIGHTLEY: Oh, as to her beauty – she always looks well. But as to her character ...

MRS WESTON: Come, Mr Knightley – with all her faults, you know she is an excellent creature.

KNIGHTLEY: Perhaps she is. But she thinks she has nothing to learn. I should like to see Emma in love, and in some doubt of a return.

MRS WESTON: Would you, really?

KNIGHTLEY: It would do her good.

John Knightley comes in, in a mood of savage enjoyment, brushing flakes of snow off his sleeve:

JOHN KNIGHTLEY: Well, the snow is lying three inches deep, and still coming down hard – a spirited beginning for your winter engagements, Mr Woodhouse!

MR WOODHOUSE: Oh! Oh, Isabella! Emma! What shall we do?

EMMA: I'm sure it's not so very bad, Papa.

JOHN KNIGHTLEY: I admired your determination in setting out, sir, and I dare say we shall get home alive. We are two carriages – if one is blown over, there will be the other at hand.

Mr Woodhouse might go into another panic at the mention of the coach blowing over.

MR WOODHOUSE: What is to be done, my dear Emma? What is to be done?

28   **EXTERIOR. RANDALLS.** *night*

It's snowing hard but not that bad; the coaches are being brought round outside.

29   **INTERIOR. RANDALLS.** *night*

The hall. Mr Woodhouse, all wrapped up, being assisted by Mr Weston and Knightley through the door. Isabella clings to John Knightley. Mr Elton looks flushed and eager.

MR ELTON: Mr Weston, Mrs Weston, how can I thank you for such a splendid evening ...

30   **INTERIOR. RANDALLS. DRAWING-ROOM.** *night*

Emma all wrapped up in her coat etc., looking again at the miniature of Frank Churchill, smiling boldly back at her. Her imagination can't resist it:

The Frank of the picture metamorphoses into a lifesize Frank Churchill, with the same bold smile, clearly very taken with Emma.

FRANK: Miss Woodhouse. We meet at last.

He bends and kisses her hand, comes up, smiling mischievously right into her eyes.

MRS WESTON: [*off*] Emma!

31   INTERIOR. RANDALLS. HALL. *night*

As Emma comes in, Mr and Mrs Weston, and an ecstatic Mr Elton, offering his arm.

MR ELTON: Mr John Knightley went in the first carriage with Mrs Knightley and your father. I am to have the pleasure of escorting you.

EMMA: Oh. Thank you.

'Oh God,' she thinks. Ten minutes of his smarmy conversation, which will probably be more boring than ever, half-cut as he is.

32   INTERIOR. CARRIAGE. *night*

Mr Elton and Emma sit opposite each other. They sit in silence for a few moments as the carriage rumbles along through the snow. Mr Elton obviously in an excited mood. Gazing ardently at Emma, who looks away every time their eyes meet. Emma feels she'd better talk.

EMMA: It seems a pity that our party had to end so ... Mr Elton!

For he has lurched forward and seized her hands.

MR ELTON: Forgive me – I must, I must avail myself of this God-given opportunity – to tell you what I am sure you must already know – that I adore you – worship you – passionately –

EMMA: Mr Elton, please ...

He's kissing her hands, her wrists ... she snatches them away, he tumbles forward almost on top of her, manages to right himself, moves to the seat beside her.

MR ELTON: Forgive me – I can't help myself – dearest Miss Woodhouse – Emma – release me from torment – tell me you return my love – tell me you will be my wife and make me the happiest man on Earth! Oh, Emma! I read my answer in your eyes!

He is about to try kissing her – she pulls away – gets on to the other seat.

EMMA: Mr Elton! I am astonished!

MR ELTON: No, no, I am sure you cannot be, lovely, lovely as you are –

Mr Elton is half-drunk and so full of self-love he thinks she's being modest. Emma's only thought is that he is so drunk he's forgotten which girl he loves, so tries to humour him:

EMMA: Mr Elton – I think you must have drunk too much of Mr Weston's good wine – you have forgot yourself – I am not Miss Smith, but I shall be happy to take any message to her.

MR ELTON: [*baffled*] Miss Smith! What should I have to do with Miss Smith? What do I care about her? Who could think of Miss Smith when Miss Woodhouse is near? [*his ardour returning*] No, no, you are all loveliness and modesty, but I am sure you could not have mistaken my intentions – no, indeed you could not!

Emma's face. She turns her face away, suddenly realizing that she might have been wrong all along. She's appalled. And for a moment really forgets he's still here. A mistake, for he launches himself upon her again:

MR ELTON: Charming Miss Woodhouse! Allow me to interpret this interesting silence! It confesses you have long understood me.

He's taking her hands again …

MR ELTON: Does it not, lovely, lovely Miss Woodhouse …

Emma fiercely, shaking him free as it were:

EMMA: No, sir, it confesses no such thing! I have seen you only as the admirer of my friend. In no other light could you have been more to me than a common acquaintance …

That's where he realizes he's made a ghastly mistake. It comes as a real shock to him. But also, she's hurt his pride with her unthinking dismissal of him as a possible suitor. [There's the class thing too.] He's her enemy from now on.

I think it's here Mr Elton would make the physical move right away, to get back his dignity as much as he can, on to the opposite seat, staring out of the window. Emma, still angry and incredulous:

EMMA: After all your attentions to Miss Smith – do you ask me to believe that you have never thought seriously of her?

Now Mr Elton is stung into answering back when he meant to keep a dignified silence.

MR ELTON: Miss Smith? I think seriously of Miss Smith? No doubt there are men who might not object – everyone has their level – but I am not, I think, quite so much at a loss. No, madam – my visits have been for yourself only – after all the encouragement I received.

EMMA: Encouragement! Sir, you have been entirely mistaken in supposing it. I have seen you only as the admirer of my friend. I am exceedingly sorry, but it's as well the mistake ends where it does.

Mr Elton, his face turned away, makes some sort of outraged 'hmmph' sort of sound.

EMMA: I trust that your … disappointment will not be lasting. I have no thoughts of matrimony at present.

Another little 'hmmph' perhaps. Jane Austen says they are both so angry that their straightforward emotions leave no room for embarrassment. Their faces. Both of them proud, angry, upset.

33   **EXTERIOR. VICARAGE/INTERIOR. CARRIAGE.** *night*

Mr Elton gets down, turns, still furious.

EMMA: Goodnight, Mr Elton.

MR ELTON: [*abrupt*] Goodnight.

Mr Elton slams the door shut. Emma sinks back against the cushions. The relief at being alone only lasts a moment.

EMMA: Oh, Harriet, Harriet!

34   EXTERIOR. HARTFIELD. *day*

The snow's gone. The John Knightleys just leaving in their carriage, children waving, 'Goodbye, Grandpapa!', Isabella waves and wipes away a tear, Emma and Mr Woodhouse at the door as the carriage moves off.

MR WOODHOUSE: Poor Isabella. She would have done much better to stay on with us. The air in London is very bad: Perry says it is most injurious. You know Emma I think Mr John Knightley one of the best of men – his manner is a little abrupt – but I think she would have done better if she had never left Hartfield. You would not do such a thing, Emma. You would never leave me.

EMMA: No, Papa.

Perhaps hear the last two sentences voice-over.

35   INTERIOR. HARTFIELD. DINING-ROOM. *day*

Emma and Mr Woodhouse one each end of the long table. The day darkening outside. Mr Woodhouse slurping tentatively at his gruel. Just little slurps, but clearly audible in the big quiet room. The servants stand patiently round. Emma's face.

36   EXTERIOR. HIGHBURY. *day*

Emma walking briskly through the village, looking serious and determined. She gets respectful greetings from the villagers as she marches through.

Emma passes on the other side of the road from the Crown Inn, and does not see the stage coach – Mr Elton's trunk being loaded up – and Mr Elton himself getting in, still looking pretty cross.

37   EXTERIOR. MRS GODDARD'S SCHOOL. *day*

The little girls are playing outside, supervised by the great girls. Harriet Smith is there, looking as lovely as ever. Emma calls to her:

EMMA: Harriet!

Harriet turns, so happy to see Emma. Emma thinks about the grim task ahead.

38   INTERIOR. MRS GODDARD'S SCHOOL. *day*

It would be nice if their conversation took place in the empty schoolroom and we could see the great girls and the small girls outside. Harriet has tears on her cheeks and in her eyes. Emma, properly remorseful, holds her hands.

EMMA: It is all my fault. Oh, Harriet, can you ever forgive me?

HARRIET: [*tremulously*] There is nothing to forgive, dear, dear Miss Woodhouse – I have nothing to complain of – I could never have deserved such a man as Mr Elton –

EMMA: No, indeed, for now I believe he doesn't deserve you. I am heartily ashamed of myself, and I am determined to mend my ways.

HARRIET: Oh, Miss Woodhouse, I am sure no one would ever blame you!

EMMA: Well, if you forgive me, I'm not entirely cast down. I was on my way to Ford's – would you like to walk there with me?

HARRIET: Oh, yes!

[NO SCENE 39]

40   EXTERIOR. HIGHBURY. MAIN STREET. *day*

We can see Harriet outside Ford's talking to the Martins, her sweet face, anxious to please, very much looking at Robert, who is ill at ease, still yearning for her, the sister Elizabeth a bit tight-lipped.

Emma is standing some way off, dawdling in front of a shop window. She is carrying a neat little parcel. Harriet leaves the Martins and skittles along to catch up Emma. She is all bright-eyed and has a parcel too.

HARRIET: Dear Miss Woodhouse! – only think! I thought I should have fainted! But they were very friendly – quite friendly, more than I should have expected – He spoke to me too, you know, he was very kind and then Elizabeth said that she was sorry not to have seen me for so long – and asked if I would care to visit them one day ... Oh, Miss Woodhouse I said I would – did I do wrong?

EMMA: No, indeed, for they do seem very decent respectable people, quite deserving of notice – if only they were in a little higher rank of life, I might be able to visit them myself ... Oh Lord. Miss Bates.

Miss Bates is actually leaning out of her first floor window, very excited:

MISS BATES: Miss Woodhouse! Forgive me! I couldn't help but see you! Jane is here! Yes! She arrived this morning! Mother and I would take it so kindly if you would step up, Miss Woodhouse, and Miss Smith, too, if you would, Miss Smith?

HARRIET: Oh! That is very kind – but –

EMMA: Thank you, Miss Bates – but we cannot stay long.

MISS BATES: Oh! Jane will be beside herself with joy!

EMMA: [*sotto voce*] I doubt it.

MISS BATES: I'll send Patty down.

HARRIET: Mrs Goddard told me that Miss Fairfax is to stay in Highbury with her aunt all summer, I have never met her – what is she like, Miss Woodhouse?

41   INTERIOR. BATES' HOUSE. *day*

As Emma and Harriet go up the stairs to the first floor apartment:

EMMA: [*confidentially*] Jane Fairfax is a penniless orphan – but she has been brought up in some style by Colonel Campbell as companion to his daughter, but now the daughter's married and so Jane must find employment. Everyone speaks highly of her – I wish her well, but I am sick of the very name of her.

HARRIET: Oh, Miss Woodhouse!

42 INTERIOR. BATES' SITTING-ROOM. *day*

The room is much smaller than the ones we've seen. It seems quite overcrowded with five people in it. Mrs Bates, Miss Bates, Emma, Harriet, Jane Fairfax. She is memorably beautiful, in a style quite different from Emma's – apparently very cool and composed, but her composure conceals great depth of feeling.

Miss Bates does most of the talking, but the camera favours Jane and Emma. We are looking at her now, as Miss Bates rabbits on:

MISS BATES: Yes, it was such a surprise because we thought that Colonel Campbell would need the carriage himself and you know he would never send dear Jane Post – but as it turned out they all went off to Ireland two days early ...

EMMA: Indeed – are the whole family gone, Miss Fairfax?

JANE: Yes, they are in –

MISS BATES: Ballycraig, you know, a very beautiful place, I fancy – Miss Campbell is married to Mr Dixon now, and so I should call her Mrs Dixon, but I always forget – We should call Miss Campbell Mrs Dixon now mother, should we not? – She is only a very little deaf, you know – She always hears what Jane says, but then Jane always speaks so distinct – Yes Mr Dixon always thought so very highly of Jane – but in the end, you know, I believe they are very happy, and both very fond of Jane – We thought she would accompany them to Ireland – Jane has heard so much of the beauty of the place, from Mr Dixon I mean ... and as Jane used to be very often walking out with them ... he is a most amiable, charming young man I believe. Jane was quite longing to go to Ireland, from his account of things!

Emma has been listening to this very bright-eyed – she smells a rat – or an affair with the interesting Mr Dixon. She looks closely at Jane Fairfax, who remains very sphinxlike, and at this first pause, Emma gets in with:

EMMA: But you did not go with them after all?

JANE: I thought it better that I should not. I shall have to earn my bread sooner or later – and I decided that the sooner I made up my mind, the less pain I should inflict – or endure.

EMMA: Mr – and Mrs Dixon must have been very disappointed.

MISS BATES: Indeed I think they must have been – nothing could have been more kind and pressing – Mr Dixon does not seem in the least backward in any attention. He is a most charming young man. Ever since the service he rendered Jane at Weymouth –

JANE: Please, Aunt!

MISS BATES: No, you will not mind me telling it to Miss Woodhouse and Miss Smith – Poor

Jane nearly met with a terrible calamity – They were out on the water in a boating party, Jane, you know, and Mr Dixon, and Miss Campbell, for thus she was then, and I think they had gone out rather far ...

Emma listening eagerly, imagines, with appropriate sea noises and sea music:

42a   EXTERIOR. SEA NEAR WEYMOUTH. *day* [*Emma's fantasy*]

A sailing boat, sailors, the three well-dressed young people; Mr Dixon very handsome in a dark passionate Irish way; Miss Campbell rather plain – she is looking ahead, shading her eyes, while Mr Dixon bends attentively towards Jane; a couple of old sea salts doing the actual sailing.

MISS BATES: [*voice-over*] ... for a squall blew up, and poor Jane, by the sudden whirling round of something or other among the sails, would have been dashed into the sea at once ...

HARRIET: [*voice-over*] Oh!

Harriet's cry blending with Jane's scream, and Mr Dixon's manly cry [and we see it happen] – Jane nearly over the side – Mr Dixon grabs at her dress and hauls her back in, and into his arms, where she rests and looks up, and they gaze into each other's eyes – inescapably, passionately doomed to an undying love ... Poor Miss Campbell turns and sees what the score is – Mr Dixon's troubled face ... [Cut back to:]

42b   INTERIOR. BATES' SITTING-ROOM. *day*

We're back with Miss Bates:

MISS BATES: And ever since we had the history of that day, I have been so fond of Mr Dixon!

HARRIET: Oh! What a shocking tale!

EMMA: But one with a happy ending.

She leaves just the tiniest hint of a question there – Jane looks back at her, seems about to reply, then looks away. We look at her lovely, troubled face, and then start to hear her voice, which is exceptionally good, full of feeling held under control, and find ourselves in:

43   INTERIOR. HARTFIELD. DRAWING-ROOM. *night*

Quite a large party. Emma, Mr Woodhouse, Knightley, Mr and Mrs Weston, Mrs Bates, Miss Bates, Harriet, and Jane Fairfax, who is seated at the piano playing and singing. Range around the faces.

Harriet amazed at such brilliance, Mr Weston nodding like a chap who knows a good song when he hears one. Knightley deeply attentive, Emma noticing this, attending herself, wryly acknowledging to herself that she's not in this class, Miss Bates looking very proud of her niece.

The song comes to an end. There's a lot of applause – Jane looks ill at ease with it.

MISS BATES: No one plays better than Jane – Mr Dixon would not allow that even his fiancée was Jane's equal ...

EMMA: [*to Knightley*] She does play – and sing – infuriatingly well.

KNIGHTLEY: I've rarely heard anything to equal her.

EMMA: Certainly not from me.

KNIGHTLEY: As you say – but you won't take the pains to aspire to true excellence. She would make a good companion for you.

EMMA: I am sure you're right – but I cannot warm to her – I don't know why – I wish I could, but I can't.

She's being straight – it's one of the nice things about Emma – her honesty.

KNIGHTLEY: Perhaps because you see in her the truly accomplished young lady you would like to be thought yourself.

This is uncomfortably accurate. Emma feels it, and decides to take it lightly.

EMMA: You will make me quite ashamed of myself.

She goes off and leaves him standing, straight up to Jane, as if determined at once to rectify her lack of warmth to Jane.

Knightley [and we] watch her speak to Jane, take her by the arm, her eager confident overtures, Jane's wary response – she leads her off to a sofa. Knightley takes pleasure in watching them, for several reasons.

Now we are with Emma and Jane:

EMMA: Mrs Weston tells me that Mr Frank Churchill was at Weymouth – would he have been there at the same time as you?

JANE: Yes, I think he was, for some of the time.

EMMA: Were you acquainted with him – did you have any conversation?

JANE: We were a little acquainted, yes.

EMMA: I have to tell you he is a young gentleman in whom I have the keenest interest – you know he is Mr Weston's son, and we expect a visit from him very soon – we have never seen him in Highbury. Tell me – what is he really like? Is he handsome?

Jane seems very reserved, giving very proper replies to Emma's eager questions.

JANE: I believe he is reckoned to be a very fine young man.

EMMA: And is he agreeable?

JANE: He is ... generally thought so.

EMMA: But what did you think of him?

JANE: When one is in company all the time, at such a place as Weymouth, it is difficult to form a just impression. I think everybody found his manners pleasing.

EMMA: [*smiling*] I see I shall have to be content with that.

44   EXTERIOR. COUNTRYSIDE. *day*

A little open carriage with Emma and Harriet. [Could we say it's spring now?] Donwell Abbey in the distance.

HARRIET: And all this is Mr Knightley's?

EMMA: Of course. There is Donwell Abbey – and all these farms belong to the Donwell estate, and everyone who lives here is a tenant of Mr Knightley's, or his servant.

HARRIET: I should never have thought one man could own so much.

The birds are twittering overhead. Harriet comes as near as she ever will to making a joke:

HARRIET: The sparrows and the skylarks don't belong to Mr Knightley, do they?

EMMA: Perhaps not, but the woodcock and the pheasant certainly do.

44a   EXTERIOR. MARTINS' FARMHOUSE. *day*

The carriage is stopped outside.

HARRIET: Don't you think it is pretty and well kept, Miss Woodhouse?

It is. Espalier apple trees on both sides of a gravel walk leading to the front door. [I guess the difficulty will be in not making it look too cute.]

EMMA: Very well kept.

HARRIET: Oh, dear – now the time is come – I feel so very strange and not quite easy about seeing the Martins after – but I must be sensible.

EMMA: Yes, you must, Harriet – tell your friends that you are only able to stay fifteen minutes – there will be no danger in that.

Harriet gets down.

HARRIET: Yes. Yes.

A moment's hesitation more, then she sets off resolutely.

EMMA: Drive on, James, to the end of the lane and turn the carriage.

45   EXTERIOR. YARD. MARTINS' FARMHOUSE. *day*

Robert Martin is in the yard mending a fence, or something physical. He turns when he hears the carriage. Here comes a posh lady in her neat little trap. It's Emma. Her view of him confirms her opinion: country bumpkin. She's high, he's low.

Robert Martin bows. She nods, coolly and graciously. His look is not friendly. He has a pretty good idea of her part in Harriet's rejection of him. The carriage goes on. He wipes his hand across his forehead and walks towards the house.

46   EXTERIOR. MARTINS' FARM. *day*

The smart little carriage waiting outside with Emma as Harriet comes running up the path. Mrs Martin, Elizabeth Martin and her younger sister stand in the doorway.

47   EXTERIOR. COUNTRY ROAD. *day*

The carriage going along. Emma and Harriet.

HARRIET: It was not quite comfortable at first – but then Mrs Martin said she thought I had grown since the summer – and we went to see the marks on the wainscot where Mr Martin measured us all, and they measured me again and Mrs Martin said I had grown a good half inch, and we were all beginning to be like ourselves again – and then just at the end, what do you think? – Mr Martin himself came in!

EMMA: And what then?

Clearly to Harriet, the event is enough in itself, he didn't have to do anything or say anything.

HARRIET: Oh – nothing – he excused himself for being dirty, and went to wash himself – and then it was time for me to come away.

Not very interesting, thinks Emma. But Harriet has clearly got something from it.

48   EXTERIOR. HARTFIELD. *day*. *[later]*

Emma gets down from the carriage and goes in.

49   INTERIOR. HARTFIELD. HALL. *day*

As Emma walks through the hall she can hear voices from the drawing room:

MR WESTON: [*out of vision*] There! Is it not just as I said?

She opens the door.

50   INTERIOR. HARTFIELD. DRAWING-ROOM. *day*

Emma's slightly blurred impression – it's all such a surprise. Mrs Weston turns smiling as she comes in, and two gentlemen sitting with Mr Woodhouse rise to their feet: Mr Weston and Frank Churchill.

MR WESTON: Miss Woodhouse – Emma – allow me to present to you my son, Mr Frank Churchill.

Frank Churchill's smiling face fills the screen. [Very much as in Emma's earlier fantasy.] Very good looking with a smiley, rather mischievous face – he looks as if he has been anticipating this meeting very keenly and he's not disappointed.

FRANK: Miss Woodhouse. We meet at last.

End of Part Two

51   INTERIOR. HARTFIELD. DRAWING-ROOM. *later*

Emma and Frank Churchill up at one end of the room. Mrs Weston with Mr Woodhouse and Mr Weston at the other end, out of earshot, but facing the young people.

FRANK: I was extremely happy to meet Mrs Weston.

Emma smiles. This is just what she would have liked him to say.

FRANK: I was sure that I would like her, from her letters – but I didn't expect to see such beauty. I had imagined – well – a tolerably well-looking woman of a certain age. I didn't expect to see a pretty young woman.

Dropping his voice at the end – he has a way of talking to Emma as if they're already friends who understand each other, which is a bit cheeky, but very agreeable.

EMMA: [*smiling*] Mr Churchill, you couldn't praise her too highly for me – but you mustn't let Mrs Weston hear you speaking of her as a pretty young woman.

FRANK: I hope I should know better. I know whom I might praise without being thought extravagant in my terms.

He is telling her she's beautiful and that he, being a very handsome young man who's seen the world and knows the score, has the right both to make an informed judgement and to communicate it, and to expect her to be interested. Frank and Emma are both on the A-list, so to speak, and they both know it.

MR WESTON: [*getting up*] I must be going. I have business at The Crown – but I need not hurry anybody else.

Frank rises.

FRANK: No, if you have business, sir – perhaps I should pay a visit which must be paid at some time – a neighbour of yours [*turning to Emma*] – the name is Fairfax – but I believe the family are called Barnes, or Bates ...?

MR WESTON: Of course we know Mrs Bates! We passed the house – Miss Bates was at the window! Miss Fairfax, of course – you met her at Weymouth. A fine girl! Call upon her, by all means.

FRANK: It is of little matter – another day would do as well ... but there was that degree of acquaintance at Weymouth which ...

Frank is making a good job of acting reluctant compliance in the face of a tedious social obligation.

MR WESTON: Oh, go today, go today. What is right to be done cannot be done too soon. If you don't call early, it will be a slight.

FRANK: [*He smiles at Emma.*] Nothing for it, then.

EMMA: You know Miss Fairfax's situation in life, what she is destined to be?

FRANK: Yes – [*rather hesitatingly*] I believe I do. [*changing tack*] I hope that you will have time to introduce me to Highbury, Miss Woodhouse, and show me all the points of interest?

Emma smiles happily. Things are looking very promising.

52   **EXTERIOR. HIGHBURY.** *day*

Emma and Frank out in town, attracting a few admiring and speculative glances. Frank looks eager, cheerful, full of a young man's energy and enthusiasm, and Emma responds to it instinctively.

EMMA: This is the Crown Inn.

FRANK: That looks a fine room on the first floor – one could hold a very good ball there I should say.

EMMA: I believe it was a ballroom many years ago.

FRANK: Then we must revive it, restore its former glory – Are you fond of dancing?

EMMA: Very fond indeed! But there are too few young people in the village now to hold a dance.

FRANK: Surely not! I am sure we shall find enough, even if we have to send out as far as Leatherhead! No – a ball there shall be, and you and I shall dance at it. And there is the Bates' house – you see I am getting to be quite at home in Highbury already.

EMMA: Did you pay your visit yesterday?

FRANK: Yes, oh yes – I was just going to mention it. I thought it would never end. Ten minutes would have sufficed, but there was no getting away – the talking aunt, you know – I was there three quarters of an hour!

EMMA: And how did you think Miss Fairfax looked?

FRANK: Oh – very ill. If ladies can be allowed to look ill. A most deplorable want of complexion.

EMMA: No, no, I won't allow that. Miss Fairfax has her own style of beauty. Perhaps it's not to your taste.

FRANK: Yes, perhaps that's it. Yes, I believe you're right.

Implying, of course, that Emma's style of beauty is much more to his taste.

EMMA: Did you see her often at Weymouth? Were you often in the same society?

FRANK: Ha! This must be Ford's! That everybody attends every day of their lives. Let's go in – and then I can prove myself a true citizen of Highbury. I must buy something at Ford's. I dare say they sell gloves?

EMMA: Oh, yes! Lay out half a guinea in Ford's, and you will be adored by all Highbury!

She smiles at him, he smiles at her, offers his arm and they cross the road and go in the shop. They like each other; they make a handsome couple; it is starting to look very promising.

53 **EXTERIOR. HIGHBURY. OUTSKIRTS.** *later*

Frank and Emma walking near Mr Elton's house.

FRANK: Wherever I go I shall say I bought these gloves at Ford's of Highbury – I never go anywhere else – no, no, I mean it – and what more delights does Highbury have in store for me?

EMMA: I fear we are coming to the end of them. Here is Mr Elton's house. It cannot be said to be handsome, but he has done his best with it. Mr Elton is the vicar, and considered by some to be a very fine young man.

FRANK: Ah, I know a good deal of Mr Elton, though I've never met him.

EMMA: Really?

FRANK: I know he is at present in Bath, and just recently engaged, and shortly to be married, to a Miss Augusta Hawkins, of Bristol, with a fortune of ten thousand pounds.

EMMA: Then you know more than I do.

FRANK: I had it from Miss Bates. Everybody is full of it – agog to see Mr Elton's bride. So this is where they will live. I think they will be very snug and happy – this is a perfectly good house, to share with the woman you truly love. A man would be a blockhead who wanted more.

He says that last sentence with real strength of feeling – as if he's thinking about his own life.

EMMA: You can say this, you who have been used to Enscombe, with every degree of luxury?

FRANK: I care nothing for Enscombe. What's the good of wealth and luxury, where there's no true happiness?

That almost seems like a private reflection, as if we're getting close to the real Frank – then he lightens up:

FRANK: Shall we make the full circle to Randalls? You see I have got my bearings.

He offers his arm and she takes it.

54   INTERIOR. RANDALLS. *day*

A room with a piano in it. Frank and Emma by the window. Mr and Mrs Weston still at the tea-table near the fire.

FRANK: This is a handsome instrument – do you play, Miss Woodhouse?

EMMA: Of course – but not very well – not nearly as well as Miss Fairfax. Have you heard her play?

FRANK: Yes, once or twice at Weymouth – she appeared to me to play well, but I know nothing of the matter myself, though one of the party always preferred Miss Fairfax's playing to that of his fiancée.

EMMA: So Mr Dixon is musical, is he?

FRANK: Yes, Mr and Mrs Dixon were the persons – I thought it a very strong proof of Miss Fairfax's excellence.

EMMA: Proof, indeed! But wasn't Miss Fairfax embarrassed at this ... preference of Mr Dixon's? And did he perhaps – prefer her in other ways too?

FRANK: I – I really cannot say.

EMMA: No – who can tell what Jane Fairfax is feeling? She is so very reserved.

Frank smiles, as if he knows just what she means.

EMMA: I could never attach myself to anyone who was so completely reserved –

FRANK: No. There is safety in reserve, but no attraction. One cannot love a reserved person.

Mr and Mrs Weston are looking very benignly at the young couple, who are getting on so well.

FRANK: Father, I believe I must go to London tomorrow.

MR WESTON: To London? Whatever for?

55   INTERIOR. HARTFIELD. *day*

Mr Woodhouse, Knightley, Mr and Mrs Weston, Emma and Harriet.

KNIGHTLEY: To get his hair cut?

Knightley's forceful manner rather scares Harriet and Mr Woodhouse.

MR WESTON: [*laughing*] I fear he has, Mr Knightley. Sixteen miles there, and sixteen miles back – I told him he was a coxcomb, but he wouldn't be dissuaded.

KNIGHTLEY: [*more to himself*] Foppery and nonsense.

MRS WESTON: All young people will have their little whims.

KNIGHTLEY: Yes, I see. Just the sort of trifling, silly fellow I took him for.

Again, he says this more to himself, or the latter part of it – he doesn't want to offend Mr Weston, but he has to say it, so he sort of mutters it as he walks away. Emma very conscious of his opinion – and she can't help sharing it, so far as the haircut is concerned.

MR WOODHOUSE: I hope he will not have it cut too short – I am very much afraid he will catch cold from it.

Knightley's quite unable to get over his extreme irritation at Frank Churchill, he's been muttering various things under his breath, and now he can hardly wait for Mr Woodhouse to finish:

KNIGHTLEY: Mr Woodhouse, you will excuse me now – I have some business which I postponed to be here – Doubtless I shall meet this young man at your party for him, Mrs Weston. I bid you all good day.

And off he goes.

56 EXTERIOR. BATES' HOUSE. *day*

A great crowd gathered in the street. A pulley has been rigged up from the second floor, and a brand new ginger pianoforte is being carefully winched up to the first floor.

WORKMEN: Steady ... steady ... take it slow ... there we go ...

57 INTERIOR. BATES' SITTING-ROOM. *day*

The window-frame has been taken out and is resting against one of the walls. Mrs Bates, awake for once, stares in stark horror as the ginger beast bobs against the empty window space.

MISS BATES: It is a pianoforte, Mother!

58 EXTERIOR. RANDALLS. *night*

Lights blazing out and light streaming from the open doorway.

Knightley's carriage arriving, Knightley getting out and turning as Emma's carriage arrives.

Knightley goes to hand Emma out of the carriage.

EMMA: This is coming as you should do – using your carriage for once, like a gentleman, instead of walking everywhere.

KNIGHTLEY: Lucky that we should arrive at the same moment, then, or you wouldn't have noticed I'm more of a gentleman than usual this evening.

EMMA: Yes, I should, I am sure I should.

KNIGHTLEY: Nonsensical girl.

All this as they're walking in ...

58a INTERIOR. RANDALLS. DRAWING-ROOM. *night*

Emma and Knightley enter. She looks around for Frank Churchill. There he is, across the room, but looking out for her, and now smiling directly at her. Knightley sees this, and it irritates him.

59 INTERIOR. RANDALLS. DINING-ROOM. *night*

Emma is sitting next to Frank Churchill. We need to be able to see, Mrs Weston, Jane

Fairfax, Miss Bates, Mr Weston, Knightley and Harriet. Miss Bates to Mrs Weston, but very much at large:

MISS BATES:　　Oh, it was the greatest surprise – and really quite the finest you could wish for – not a grand, but a large-sized square one! A very elegant-looking instrument – and it arrived just yesterday, without any direction! Jane herself was quite at a loss who could have sent it!

HARRIET:　　What a mystery!

MISS BATES:　　Ah, but now we conclude it could only be from one quarter, do we not, Jane, for who else could it be from but Colonel Campbell?

Jane with lowered eyes trying not to be part of this.

FRANK:　　[*to Emma*] What are they talking about?

EMMA:　　It seems that some mysterious person has made Miss Fairfax a present of a pianoforte.

[*Miss Bates can be heard going on in the background while we are listening to Frank and Emma.*]

MISS BATES:　　I declare, I don't know when I've heard anything that gave me more satisfaction. Well I must say I used to play as a girl but never you know so well as Jane ... but now she has the new one there will be no stopping her ...

EMMA:　　[*to Frank*] Why do you smile?

FRANK:　　Nay, why do you? I smile because you smile. Why, do you suspect something? If Colonel Campbell is not the giver, who can be?

EMMA:　　What do you say to Mr Dixon?

They are both speaking quietly and looking at Jane, who is very conscious of being looked at and talked about.

EMMA:　　I can't help suspecting that he might have had the misfortune to fall in love with her.

FRANK:　　You're sure it couldn't have been the Colonel?

EMMA:　　[*shaking her head*] If it had been the Colonel, she would have guessed at once, and not been puzzled.

Jane looks at them for a moment, her face troubled.

Emma turns in triumph to Frank.

EMMA:　　I have no doubt at all – it was an offering of love.

FRANK:　　An offering of love. You have convinced me. I believe it was.

He smiles – she smiles – Emma thinks they are two brilliant detectives. Frank smiles across at Jane too, and she turns her face away from him.

60　　**INTERIOR. RANDALLS. DRAWING-ROOM.** *night*

Emma is playing and singing – Frank in attendance to turn the pages. Emma plays and sings very well within her limitations – she sticks to simple folk songs. It might be nice if

she has mischievously chosen one that alludes to boats, like 'Speed Bonny Boat', or 'To Love and Ireland'. So she can smile up at Frank, and he can smile knowingly back. She smiles at Knightley too, who smiles back — he always likes to hear Emma sing and to admire her appearance.

Rather surprising Emma, Frank joins in, harmonizing in a light baritone — see Knightley's lip curl, or something. 'Jumped up little show-off,' he thinks.

The song ends, people clap.

MR WESTON: Encore! Encore!

EMMA: No, no, I thank you, but you have heard quite enough of me!

They surrender their places.

KNIGHTLEY:	Miss Fairfax, would you give us the great pleasure of hearing you?
JANE:	Yes, if you wish, Mr Knightley.

She moves to the piano.

MR PERRY:	[*sitting next to Harriet*] Ah, Miss Smith. Keeping well, I trust – no more throats?
HARRIET:	[*pleased to be spoken to*] Oh no, Mr Perry. I'm very well now, thank you.

Jane plays and sings an Italian song. Much more demanding technically, but also something that enables her to express deep emotion – perhaps this is the way this secretive reserved girl finds an outlet for her feelings.

Knightley, as before, listening intently with great pleasure.

Frank slips into a seat next to Emma on the other side of the room.

FRANK:	I shall have been here a week tomorrow. Half my time. I never knew days fly so fast.
EMMA:	Perhaps you now regret spending one of them in getting your hair cut.
FRANK:	No, that is no subject of regret. Not at all ...

He seems to have lost his thread, staring abstractly in Jane Fairfax's direction.

EMMA:	What's the matter?
FRANK:	[*coming to*] Oh – I was struck by – really Miss Fairfax has done her hair in so very odd a way – I never saw anything so *outrée*. I must go and ask her whether it's an Irish fashion. Shall I?
EMMA:	[*laughing*] No, no, you shouldn't.
FRANK:	Yes, I will – and you shall see how she takes it – see whether she blushes.

As he's on his way over, Jane finishes the song, and Knightley gets up to go over and congratulate her.

We can see Jane smiling up at Knightley, giving him a real smile, before Frank claims her attention, making her start another song, in which, after a while, he joins in. Knightley's expression changes whenever Frank is singing. Clearly he prefers to listen to Jane singing alone – or is that all it is?

Meanwhile Mrs Weston slips into the seat next to Emma.

MRS WESTON:	I have been making discoveries, Emma. Did you know that Miss Bates and Miss Fairfax came here in Mr Knightley's own carriage? And are to go home the same way? Isn't that a very marked attention – from Mr Knightley, who never uses his carriage for himself?
EMMA:	Yes it is – but just the sort of kindness I'd expect of him. He is not a gallant man – but he is a very humane one.
MRS WESTON:	Hmm. What do you say to – Mr Knightley and Miss Fairfax?
EMMA:	Oh, no! And cut my little nephew Henry out of inheriting Donwell? Never. Besides, he doesn't care about Jane Fairfax. In the way of love, I am sure he does not.

But it looks a possibility: at the moment Knightley is gazing steadily, earnestly at Jane, who is resisting Frank's efforts to make her stay at the piano.

MRS WESTON:	He is a great admirer of her talents – what if he should have sent for this pianoforte?

Knightley has lost his patience with Frank Churchill. His decisive tones ring across the room, silencing everyone.

KNIGHTLEY:	My dear sir, I must intervene. If Miss Fairfax says she is tired, we should have the courtesy to believe her. Would you have her sing herself hoarse?

Knightley, conscious of people listening, says more gently:

KNIGHTLEY:	Come, Miss Fairfax, you have earned a rest.

Jane looking up at him gratefully:

JANE:	Thank you.

Emma notices this – could Mrs Weston be right? But now Frank comes over, holding out his hand for Emma to take.

FRANK:	Miss Woodhouse, I have come here determined to dance, and nothing will satisfy me but that you and I shall show the way. Will you?
EMMA:	With pleasure.

Dissolve into Frank and Emma dancing together, very lively and energetic, Harriet in the dancing too, quite happy, Knightley watching. What's he thinking? We don't know.

61   INTERIOR. STAIRWAY. BATES' HOUSE. *day*

Miss Bates leading Emma and Harriet up the stairs.

MISS BATES: So obliged to you for your visit – Jane will be so pleased to show you the new instrument – Mr Frank Churchill is here already, fastening the rivet of my mother's spectacles, he really is so very – Pray take care, Miss Woodhouse, remember the step at the turning, remember the step, Miss Smith, the step at the turning ...

62   INTERIOR. BATES' SITTING-ROOM. *day*

Mrs Bates, asleep by the fire. Jane Fairfax sitting at the piano leafing through some music. Frank has just moved from the piano to the table, where he has the spectacles. Does he look just a teeny bit flustered? The old lady gives a little snore.

Jane Fairfax turns, rises, and gives a little smile and bow.

FRANK: Ah – this is a pleasure. You find me occupied in trying to be useful. The pianoforte would not stand steady. You see we have been wedging it with paper. Will you try it now, Miss Fairfax – just a few notes?

She smiles, sits down, then starts to play a simple waltz tune.

FRANK: Ah, yes! You hear that softness in the upper notes – just what those in Mr Dixon's party particularly prized.

We can see Jane's face, though Frank and Emma can't. She smiles to herself – not a mischievous smile, like Frank's, but a tender one.

FRANK: Mr Dixon I believe valued that tone particularly.

Now we are on Frank and Emma.

EMMA: [*whispers*] It isn't fair. Don't distress her.

Jane stops playing.

FRANK: What felicity to hear that tune again! If I mistake not, that was danced at Weymouth!

She looks at him, looks quickly away. Starts to play something else. Frank picks up some music.

FRANK: Here's something new. A set of Irish melodies. That was thoughtful of whoever sent the instrument. That betokens true affection, I believe.

Here again, we see Jane's tender expression. Clearly Mr Dixon, or whoever it was, still holds a very important place in Jane's affections too.

She plays on.

Miss Bates is beaming placidly. Harriet is looking in amazement at Jane's nimble fingers.

FRANK: But I'm forgetting – our ball is arranged for next Saturday at the Crown – my father is all enthusiasm – I have received permission from Enscombe to extend my stay, so I shall hope to see you all there – and Miss Woodhouse – I hope it is not too soon to secure you for the first two dances of the evening?

Emma smiles.

Frank smiles. Harriet wide-eyed, an eager spectator at this posh romance. Jane plays on.

[NO SCENE 63]

64   INTERIOR. HARTFIELD. *day*

Emma is reading in the window-seat looking over the rear garden. Mr Woodhouse is taking a nap by the fire.

A knock on the front door makes Emma look up. [Sound of doors opening and closing, off,] and then a servant comes in, sees that Mr Woodhouse is asleep, and consequently says softly:

SERVANT: Mr Churchill, ma'am.

Frank Churchill comes in. He looks uncharacteristically agitated, and is about to speak, when Emma, who has jumped up, puts her finger to her lips, smiling, and indicating Mr Woodhouse. She beckons Frank over to the window-seat. [This means that the conversation has to be conducted in near-whispers.]

FRANK: I come as the bearer of evil tidings – for me they are. Mrs Churchill is ill – I must leave immediately for Enscombe.

EMMA: I am very sorry to hear it – I hope it is not very severe?

FRANK: Who can tell? But it would seem that she is far too unwell to do without me. I dare say I shall arrive at Enscombe and find her quite recovered. But you see how it is – I cannot refuse to go.

EMMA: No, of course you cannot.

He sits lost in thought for a moment or two – he seems really quite upset – quite unlike his usual self.

FRANK: Of all horrid things, leave-taking is the worst.

EMMA: But you will come again – this will not be your only visit to Highbury.

He sighs.

EMMA: I suppose our poor ball must be quite given up.

FRANK: For the present – but if and when I get away, we shall have it ... [*He looks up at her.*] Don't forget your engagement.

EMMA: No, I promise you that. The first two dances.

FRANK: It has been ... such a fortnight. Every day more precious than the day before. Every day ... making me less fit to bear any other place.

His words, and the feeling with which he says them, seem a bit in excess of what's required. After all, he hasn't declared his love yet. So Emma might find it a little curious.

EMMA: And you must be off this very morning?

FRANK: Yes, my father is to join me here, we shall walk back together, and I must be off immediately.

EMMA: Not five minutes to spare even for Miss Fairfax and Miss Bates?

FRANK: Oh yes – I have called there – passing the door, I thought it the right thing to do. I went in for three minutes, but Miss Bates was out – and I felt I should wait till she came in. [*tiny abstracted pause*] I ...

He pauses again – looks directly into Emma's eyes.

FRANK: In short ... perhaps, Miss Woodhouse – I think you can hardly be quite without suspicion ...?

A very pregnant pause. Is he going to tell her he's fallen in love with her? He seems to be waiting for some sign from her. Then there's a knock on the front door again.

FRANK: Ah – this will be my father. Better not to disturb Mr Woodhouse. I ... hope we shall meet again before too long.

I wonder if he might kiss her hand, rather hastily – it's quite a moving moment – if not, it's a look and a bow, not at all like his usual self-possessed easy manner.

EMMA: Goodbye.

He turns and goes.

End of Part Three

[NO SCENE 65]

66 EXTERIOR. HIGHBURY. *day*

Some nice pompous music for Mrs Elton's arrival on the scene: she and Mr Elton ride through Highbury in an open carriage like royalty – Mr Elton raising his hat to people he knows, Mrs Elton nodding graciously.

67 EXTERIOR. ELTONS' HOUSE. *day*

Servants carrying in Mrs Elton's gear – we can hear her carrying on inside [we might just get a glimpse of her at the window]:

MRS ELTON: No, no, no, the piano must go there – and the bookcases so – just as they are at Maple Grove! Now – Knightley and Woodhouse are the pick of the local gentry I suppose, with Weston a little behind? It's a very small place, Mr E, it will take some getting used to – Mind the fire-irons!

68 INTERIOR. HARTFIELD. DRAWING-ROOM. *day*

Mrs Elton is talking to, or at, Emma, who listens politely. [In the book Harriet isn't there, but I'd like to have her there to listen.]

Mr Elton is at the other side of the room, ostensibly talking to Mr Woodhouse, but sending many proud and loving gazes across at Mrs Elton. She is a handsome woman, with strong traces of a Bristol accent, and a very good opinion of herself.

MRS ELTON:	Why! I could almost fancy myself at Maple Grove – my brother-in-law Mr Suckling's seat, you know – the morning room there is just such a shape and size as this – Mr E!
MR ELTON:	Yes, my love?
MRS ELTON:	Is this room not astonishingly like the morning room at Maple Grove?
MR ELTON:	Very like indeed, Augusta – no one observes things as you do.
MRS ELTON:	I am extremely partial to Maple Grove. My brother and sister will be enchanted with this place! The grounds, you know – people with extensive grounds are always pleased with anything in the same style.
EMMA:	When you've seen more of the country, you may think you've overrated Hartfield. Surrey is full of beauties.
MRS ELTON:	Oh, yes! I am aware of that. It is the garden of England, you know. Surrey is the garden of England.
EMMA:	[*smiling*] Many counties I believe are called the garden of England.
HARRIET:	[*shy whisper*] Kent – and Evesham too.
MRS ELTON:	[*with a satisfied smile*] No, I fancy not. I never heard any county but Surrey called so. My brother and sister have promised us a visit in the summer – they will have their barouche-landau, of course, which holds four perfectly – and we shall be able to explore all the beauties of the countryside – we explored to King's Weston that way most delightfully – just after their first having the barouche-landau. But you will have many parties of that kind I suppose, Miss Woodhouse?
EMMA:	No, not many – we are a very quiet set of people, I believe.
MRS ELTON:	Well, we must do something about that, must we not, Mr E? We have been calling at Randalls, and very pleasant people they seem to be. Mr Weston seems an excellent creature – quite a first-rate favourite with me already, I assure you. And Mrs Weston – she was your governess I think! I was astonished to find her so ladylike. Quite the gentlewoman!

Emma open-mouthed.

MRS ELTON:	And who do you think came in while we were there? Knightley! Knightley himself! My caro sposo had spoken of 'My friend Knightley' – well, I declare he need not be ashamed of his friend. Knightley is quite the gentleman. I like him very much. And Jane Fairfax! I quite rave about poor Jane Fairfax, and I resolved to do what I can for her – I shall look out for a situation for her as a governess – if we can bring her out a little, she might even do for Maple Grove – might she not, Mr E? And I dare say we shall sometimes find room for her in the barouche-landau!

69   EXTERIOR. HARTFIELD. *day*

The garden. It's warm weather now – it might be amusing if Emma and Mrs Weston are strolling on the lawn in summer frocks, while Mr Woodhouse is sitting on the terrace with a shawl round his shoulders and a rug on his knees. Mr Weston with him. Knightley starts on the terrace, then moves down.

Emma is talking to Mrs Weston, and being partly overheard:

EMMA: Insufferable woman! With her caro sposo and her Mr E! Actually to discover that Mr Knightley is a gentleman!

MR WOODHOUSE: [*to Mr Weston*] I thought her a very pretty sort of young lady, though she speaks a little too quick. But no doubt she will make him a good wife. Though I think he had better not have married.

MR WESTON: Come, come, Mr Woodhouse, you mustn't be an enemy to every marriage.

EMMA: [*continuing to Mrs Weston*] And poor Miss Fairfax, whatever her faults, has not deserved this! To be pitied and patronized by such a person! And now she must spend almost every day with the Eltons! With her taste, and her pride! How could she endure it?

Knightley has wandered nearer.

MRS WESTON: Perhaps it is better than being always at home?

KNIGHTLEY: You are right, Mrs Weston. Miss Fairfax might well prefer to be invited by others. But she receives attentions from Mrs Elton which no one else pays her. She deserves better.

This is a pointed rebuke to Emma – and she feels it. She knows she ought to invite Jane, but she doesn't like her much, so she neglects her.

EMMA: I know how highly you think of Jane Fairfax.

This is almost like one of Miss Bingley's lines from Pride and Prejudice *– and Knightley's reply, dead straight to her teasing tone, is very like one of Darcy's put-downs.*

KNIGHTLEY: Yes. Anybody may know how highly I think of her.

Emma's face. A little bit alarmed. In her imagination:

70   **INTERIOR. CHURCH.** *day. [Emma's fantasy]*

Jane Fairfax smiles up at Knightley as he holds the ring, about to slip it on her finger. Emma's face, in the aisle, horrified. She has Henry at her side.

EMMA: But what about little Henry?

Everybody turns to look at her.

71   **INTERIOR. HARTFIELD.** *night*

Emma wakes from this dream, and sits up in bed. Smiles with relief when she realizes it's only a dream.

7 1 a   EXTERIOR. COUNTRY LANE. *day*

Emma and Harriet walking.

HARRIET: I have been thinking – forgive me Miss Woodhouse – but are you very sad that Mr Frank Churchill has had to go away? I had thought that –

EMMA: [*laughing*] Yes, so did I, Harriet – but I find I bear his absence very well. I believe I've enjoyed every moment I've spent in his company – but I suspect he's … not necessary to my happiness.

If from that we soar up above these two girls walking down the country lane, we can see not far off:

Knightley and Robert Martin riding at walking pace along the road – another road – they can see the girls but the girls can't see them. They've been to market. Knightley sees Robert look at Harriet, then away, sad.

KNIGHTLEY: Come, Robert. More fish in the sea, you know.

Robert doesn't see it like that.

ROBERT MARTIN: Not for me, Mr Knightley.

KNIGHTLEY: Well, well. [*pause, then vigorously*] Some young women ought to have more to do than meddle where they have no business!

Robert thinks what? Knightley clears his throat, and they ride on.

7 2   INTERIOR. HARTFIELD. DINING-ROOM. *day*

A dinner party. Emma, Mr Woodhouse, Mr Elton, Mrs Elton, Mrs Weston, Mr Knightley, Jane Fairfax.

MRS ELTON: Now, Jane, you shall not escape me! Here is April come, and June will soon be here – I get quite anxious about you – have you really heard of nothing? A situation such as you deserve is no everyday occurrence! You have already missed the opportunity with Mrs Bragge …

[Mrs Elton explains the unique excellence of Mrs Bragge to the whole table.]

MRS ELTON: … A cousin of Mr Suckling of Maple Grove! The whole world was dying to be governess in that family! Wax candles in the schoolroom – you may imagine how desirable! But let us not lose hope! We must begin enquiring for you directly!

JANE: I beg you would not, Mrs Elton. There are places in town where enquiry would soon produce employment. Offices for the sale … not quite of human flesh – but of human intellect.

Jane clearly feels oppressed and distressed by Mrs Elton's officious interest, and sadly stoical about her fate. Knightley looks keenly sympathetic. Emma noticing his expression.

MRS ELTON: Oh! My dear! You quite shock me, if you mean a fling at the slave trade!

JANE: No, no. The governess-trade was all I had in view. Different as to the guilt of those who carry it on – but as to the greater misery of the victims, I am not sure where it lies.

That bleak, though witty, revelation of unhappiness silences everyone for a moment or two. Jane lowers her eyes. Mrs Elton recovers first, leaning across to speak to Emma, a confidence that can be heard by the whole table.

MRS ELTON: What a dear old creature your father is – I assure you I like him excessively. I wish you could hear the gallant speeches he has been making to me all through dinner – I began to think my caro sposo would be absolutely jealous!

Mr Elton is beaming proudly: his wife can do no wrong. Emma shocked into silence. Mr Woodhouse himself baffled by this.

MRS ELTON: Ah! Look at him now! All innocence! [*stage whisper*] I fancy I am rather a favourite.

I guess the tone is rather like that grisly way some nursing staff sometimes talk in front of old people in a geriatric ward. The door opens and a servant announces:

SERVANT: Mr Weston.

Mr Weston comes in, all brisk and excited. People are getting up.

EMMA: Mr Weston, have you dined? Come and sit down.

MR WESTON: No, no, don't disturb yourselves, yes I have dined – I am just returned from London, and I walked straight round here – My dear, Frank is coming again – next week – the whole family – milder air, you know, for Mrs Churchill – they have taken a house at Richmond – he'll be able to ride over every day – Well, Emma, this is good news for you – you shall have your ball at the Crown after all!

73 **EXTERIOR. CROWN INN.** *night*

See the exterior of the building, carriages outside, people still going in, and hear the first bars of the introduction to the first dance, and then cut to:

74 **INTERIOR. CROWN INN.** *night*

Emma and Frank Churchill about to begin the first dance, at the head of the line – he bows, she curtseys, as they come up, their eyes meet, his amused, penetrating gaze, her happy smile, and the dance begins ... then Knightley watching, something about Frank's assured air doesn't appeal to him ...

MISS BATES:	This is admirable! Excellently contrived, upon my word – nothing lacking. Could not have imagined it. Jane, Jane, look – did you ever see anything like it?

Jane turns from watching Frank and Emma and gives Miss Bates a little smile.

Knightley turns away to be polite to Miss Bates and Jane Fairfax.

Mrs Elton is talking to Mr Weston and Mrs Weston about Frank.

MRS ELTON:	A very fine young man indeed, Mr Weston. You may believe me. I never compliment – so truly the gentleman, without the least conceit or puppyism. I am extremely pleased with him.
MR WESTON:	Thank you, Mrs Elton. I have yet to meet anyone who did not like my son.
MRS ELTON:	Ah, but you must know that I can be very severe upon young men – I have a vast dislike of puppies, quite a horror of them – had he turned out to be a puppy I might have said some very cutting things, you may be sure – I am a scourge of puppies, am I not, Mr E?
MR ELTON:	Indeed you are, Augusta – woe betide any puppy who ventures into your society!

The Eltons turn to each other in an ecstasy of mutual satisfaction, and Mr and Mrs Weston contrive to slip away as we dissolve into:

[Later:] Emma still dancing with Frank, Harriet dancing with some middle-aged gentleman … Emma notices that Knightley is standing in a group of older men, including Mr Perry, he stands out amongst them – tall, erect, distinguished, a fine physical animal, his gaze remains on Jane Fairfax, then Emma – she smiles, but his gaze remains serious … Frank often whispers to Emma and makes her laugh, and often laughs across at Jane Fairfax who returns his gaze serenely. All the important stuff in this sequence is what is going on with Emma, Jane Fairfax, Knightley, and Frank Churchill, but that is all movement and looks, so let's have Miss Bates as background noise:

MISS BATES:	[going straight on] Oh Mr Weston you must really have had Aladdin's lamp – good Mrs Stokes would never know her room again. I saw her just now, you know – 'Did you not wet your feet,' she said, 'coming from the carriage?' 'No we did

not,' I said, 'did we Jane?' There was a mat you know. Mr Frank Churchill was so extremely – and there he is dancing – Good evening, Mr Knightley – Mr Churchill cuts a very fine figure, does he not, Mr Knightley?

KNIGHTLEY: Very sprightly.

MISS BATES: Very sprightly, yes indeed, that is the word for him and so well partnered in Miss Woodhouse they make a very pretty pair, do they not, Jane, they might have been made to stand up together –

JANE: Yes, Aunt.

Mr and Mrs Weston exchange a glance – that's just what they feel … Perhaps Jane Fairfax might walk away at this point? So hard to do it without giving the game away. Knightley, of course, doesn't like Frank Churchill, so he won't look pleased. Now Emma looks across at Knightley, and smiles warmly, affectionately. He's glad that she did – he melts a bit, and her smile broadens.

[Dissolve into another dance:] Emma is dancing with Mr Weston. Frank dancing with Jane, though he often smiles across to Emma as though sharing a joke, when Jane isn't looking, but he is being very attentive to Jane too, and Jane is a good dancer, light and graceful – when she smiles she's really lovely. Poor Harriet is sitting out and looking rather disconsolate. She is the only girl with no partner. Emma is able to observe the following: Mr Elton is sauntering about – very near Harriet, though he disdains to notice her. Mrs Weston comes up to him.

MRS WESTON: Do you not dance, Mr Elton?

MR ELTON: [*horribly gallant*] Most readily, Mrs Weston, if you will dance with me.

MRS WESTON: Me! Oh! no – I would get you a better partner.

MR ELTON: If Mrs Gilbert wishes to dance it would give me very great pleasure, I'm sure.

MRS WESTON: Mrs Gilbert does not mean to dance – but here is a young lady disengaged – Miss Smith.

MR ELTON: Miss Smith! I am much obliged to you. I did not notice Miss Smith. But I am an old married man now. My dancing days are over. You will excuse me, Mrs Weston.

He does that in the most insensitive way, not caring whether Harriet hears or not [she does] and the way he looks at her is utterly disdainful. He strolls off towards Knightley.

MR ELTON: Ah! Mr Knightley!

KNIGHTLEY: Excuse me, sir.

Knightley walks off leaving Mr Elton with egg on his face, goes straight up to Harriet, who is all red in the face and on the verge of bursting into tears. He bends over Harriet – we don't hear his words – it's all in the moves and looks and the astonished glances of Mr and Mrs Elton.

Harriet looks up, all radiant and grateful suddenly, and he leads her to the dance. And they dance very well. Emma is pleased, Mrs Weston is pleased, Mr Weston is pleased, but Knightley gives his full attention to Harriet, just as he should.

[Dissolve to:] the end of that dance. Knightley leading Harriet back to her place – again we don't hear what they're saying, but he is obviously being very warm and friendly and she is gazing up into his face eagerly ... Mrs Elton observes sneeringly:

MRS ELTON: I see Knightley has taken pity on poor little Miss Smith! Very good natured, I declare!

Would it be good if Knightley heard this and gave her a cool look of disapprobation? Now if two other girls speak to Harriet and she turns to them, it frees Knightley to turn to Emma, who comes up smiling:

EMMA: That was well done.

KNIGHTLEY: I think they aimed at wounding more than Harriet. Why are they your enemies, Emma? – Well, perhaps I can guess, in Mr Elton's case. Confess, Emma – you did want him to marry Harriet.

EMMA: I did, and they cannot forgive me. I admit now I was completely mistaken in Mr Elton. There is a littleness about him which you discovered and I did not.

KNIGHTLEY: Well, in my turn I'll admit I underestimated Harriet Smith – she has some first-rate qualities which Mrs Elton is totally without.

We can see Mrs Elton carrying on about this or that. Knightley turns to look at Harriet and says with some strength of feeling:

KNIGHTLEY: An unpretending, single-minded, artless girl – infinitely to be preferred by any man of sense and taste to such a woman as Mrs Elton.

As he speaks, Harriet turns, and smiles at them both. The orchestra strikes up again, and Mr Weston bustles up.

MR WESTON: Come, Miss Woodhouse, Miss Otway, Miss Smith, what are you all doing? Come, Emma, set your companions the example!

EMMA: I am ready.

KNIGHTLEY: Who will you dance with?

She hesitates a second, then:

EMMA: With you, if you will ask me.

KNIGHTLEY: [*offering his hand*] Will you?

EMMA: Indeed I will.

As they move towards the dance:

EMMA: I've seen how well you dance now – and we're not really so much brother and sister as to make it improper.

KNIGHTLEY: Brother and sister! No, indeed.

And if this dance is quite a merry mingling sort of one – so if everyone's on the floor – Frank exchanging knowing smiles with Emma, Harriet reserving most of her smiles for Knightley, but getting some looks from Frank too, Knightley looking with respect and admiration every time he's with Jane Fairfax, we can create a nice little flurry about who's going to get who in the end.

75   **EXTERIOR. COUNTRY ROAD.** *day*

Highbury outskirts. Harriet and a friend from the school – Miss Otway – we've seen her with Harriet at the dance, and in church – are walking along twittering happily about the dance.

HARRIET: No, no, I don't think him old at all – when you talk to him he seems quite different – but I was very surprised at first.

Gypsies on higher ground – their point-of-view of the two plump little chicks on the road below. A stout woman and three or four ragged barefoot little kids with dirty faces.

Down below, Miss Otway says something in Harriet's ear and they both burst out laughing:

HARRIET: No, no! You are not to think that!

GYPSY WOMAN: Go on then.

The kids run down the slope and start harassing the girls.

GYPSY KIDS: Pretty lady, pretty lady, gis a penny, pretty lady, we'm all starving, only a penny, please, pretty lady ...

Harriet and Miss Otway walk faster. They are a bit panicky about this. The kids are surrounding them now, more kids and women are coming down the slope. One kid pulls at Miss Otway's arm, scaring her:

MISS OTWAY: No! Leave us alone! Come, Harriet!

And she starts to run, really fast, completely panicked. Harriet decides she'd better follow, but turns her ankle almost immediately – she can't stand on it – she sinks down ... they are all surrounding her.

HARRIET: Please ... please ...

She opens her purse to take out a coin. Little grubby hands are diving into the purse for more coins.

Frank Churchill, coming round the bend on horseback, sees the scene and kicks his horse up:

FRANK: What the devil d'ye do here? Stand away from that lady!

The gypsy woman and kids run away up the slope, and Frank leaps off his horse, and lifts Harriet.

FRANK: Why, Miss Smith!

HARRIET: [*faintly*] Mr Churchill!

She faints in his arms.

76   INTERIOR. HARTFIELD. HALL. *day*

Harriet half lying on a sofa. Emma is sponging her scrapes and bruises. A servant standing by. Frank walking back and forth, looking devilish handsome in his riding boots and breeches.

FRANK: The most extraordinary good fortune I happened to come at that moment – I was just on my way to return a pair of scissors to Miss Bates. God knows what might have happened if I hadn't ...

EMMA: It does seem like Providence – or something in a romance, full of brigands and outlaws ... But for this to happen in Highbury ...

HARRIET: How can I ever thank you enough, Mr Churchill?

FRANK: I'm happy to have been of service, Miss Smith.

Emma's gaze moves from one to the other. And imagines:

77   EXTERIOR. MRS GODDARD'S SCHOOL. *day*.
[*Emma's fantasy*]

Harriet with great girls and small girls turns to see Frank Churchill galloping up on a splendid horse; she runs towards him, and without breaking pace, he leans down and scoops her up; she gives a little squeal; and he places her in front of him on the horse ...

FRANK: Giddup!

And he carries her away triumphantly, waving his hat above his head. All the little girls are jumping up and down, and the great girls are waving their handkerchiefs.

78   EXTERIOR. DONWELL ABBEY. *day*

Very early morning. Donwell Abbey shimmers in the mist. It should be pretty breathtaking.

MRS ELTON: [*voice-over*] Mr Knightley requests the pleasure of your company on Saturday June 4th at Donwell Abbey, to taste his strawberries – which are ripening fast.

Now we see Knightley and his guests roaming the grounds – maybe from above at first – all these ladies and gentlemen looking a bit incongruous – nature clashing with culture – a bit Discreet Charm of the Bourgeoisie – and Mrs Elton's dress would probably clash with the colours of Nature. She has a huge shepherdess hat, and carries a basket with ribbons on her arm.

MRS ELTON: Quite delightful, Knightley – everything simple and natural, just as I like it. No form or parade – we shall be just like gypsies!

Harriet, overhearing, looks a bit alarmed.

KNIGHTLEY: Not in every respect, I trust.

MRS ELTON: I wish we had come on a donkey – Miss Bates and I – with my caro sposo walking by – nothing could be more natural than that, I suppose.

Miss Bates looks alarmed at this idea.

KNIGHTLEY: Some might consider it so, madam.

Emma is nearly bursting out laughing.

MRS ELTON: But Knightley you should have left all to me – the invitations, everything – I should have been glad to be Lady Patroness – it would have been no trouble to me.

KNIGHTLEY: Perhaps not, but there is only one woman I could ever allow to invite what guests she pleased to Donwell.

MRS ELTON: [*miffed*] Mrs Weston, I suppose.

KNIGHTLEY: No. Mrs Knightley.

Emma's startled look. Does he have a Mrs Knightley in mind?

KNIGHTLEY: And until she is in being I will manage such matters myself.

78a   EXTERIOR. WALLED GARDEN. DONWELL ABBEY. *day*

KNIGHTLEY: Well – here we are – you are all very welcome.

The strawberry beds. The guests spread out along the beds, bending over them, picking strawberries, separating into little groups, while the sun climbs high overhead. We can hear Mrs Elton and Miss Bates overlapping each other:

MRS ELTON: Oh, the finest fruit in England –

MISS BATES: I believe they're everybody's favourite – always wholesome –

MRS ELTON: How delightful to gather for oneself – the only way to really enjoy them, don't you think, with one's basket over one's arm ... so simple and natural, I fancy myself as a sort of shepherdess you know ...

MISS BATES:	Oh, are you fond of sheep then, Mrs Elton?
MRS ELTON:	Morning's definitely the best time to gather –
MISS BATES:	The price of strawberries in London –
MRS ELTON:	... this strawberry picking can be very tiring in this heat ...
MISS BATES:	Yes, I was just saying to Jane, I do believe one can have one too many ...
MRS ELTON:	Of course I have always thought red currants are far superior –
MISS BATES:	Yes, they are very good – and raspberries too – gooseberries, you know, and plums – and then the apples and the pears ... I don't –
MRS ELTON:	This heat is really intolerable!
MISS BATES:	Oh! Indeed, very lucky with the weather ... must go and sit in the shade.
MRS ELTON:	To speak the truth I am heartily sick of strawberries!

But their words could go for most people – brows are beginning to sweat and backs to ache. Baskets are full.

78b   EXTERIOR. DONWELL GARDENS AND HOUSES. *day*

People are lolling rather inelegantly on chairs under the trees, mopping their brows. Mrs Weston comes out to Emma.

EMMA:	How is my father? Is he asking for me?
MRS WESTON:	He will do very well for a little while.
EMMA:	I thought Mr Churchill was to be with us today.
MRS WESTON:	He hoped to ride over from Richmond. I am anxious – I have fears of his horse.
EMMA:	More likely Mrs Churchill has produced some new symptom to keep him with her. Look. Poor Jane Fairfax.

Mrs Elton is haranguing Jane Fairfax, out of earshot.

EMMA:	How can she bear it? [*after a few moments*] I think I should walk back to the house to see how Papa does.

And she goes, leaving Mrs Weston under the tree. As she nears Mrs Elton and Jane:

MRS ELTON:	Now I really will not take no for an answer – this is a friend of Mrs Bragge, a very superior situation, with only two daughters – and very close to Maple Grove – say the word, Jane, and I shall write this very day.
JANE:	I beg you would excuse me, Mrs Elton.

She is going off, but Emma, on a kind impulse, approaches her.

EMMA:	Miss Fairfax? Are you quite well? Is there anything I can do? This heat is really most oppressive. Will you go into the house with me?
JANE:	Miss Woodhouse. I think I must go home. I am quite well – but I think I must ... make sure my grandmother lacks nothing – will you be so kind as to say that, when I am missed?
EMMA:	Yes – but let me order our carriage for you, it can be here in five minutes.

JANE: No – please – the greatest kindness you can show me will be to let me have my own way, and only say I am gone when it is necessary. Will you do that?

EMMA: Yes, of course, if you wish it.

JANE: Thank you. Oh, Miss Woodhouse, the comfort of being sometimes alone!

And she goes.

Emma walks back towards the house – people are dispersed all round the grounds now – and on her way she sees Harriet and Knightley walking tête à tête, so absorbed in their conversation they don't see her at all.

In the distance, on a path, Jane Fairfax and Frank Churchill appear to be having an altercation. She is walking on, he is remonstrating, she turns round on him, he marches off in the direction of the house. This Emma does not see. We might see it in the background, behind her, as she walks in the other direction.

79   INTERIOR. DONWELL ABBEY. HALL. *day*

Emma comes in – it should feel very cool and spacious inside – not daunting at all, despite its size, something of a bachelor's house. A big dog pads around after her. This is a nice place, she thinks. I like it here.

79a   INTERIOR. DONWELL ABBEY. LIBRARY. *day*

Here's Mr Woodhouse in the library, poring over a case of butterflies. There is a big fire going. Emma and dog look in from the door.

MR WOODHOUSE: Ah, there you are, my dear. I hope you are being careful as to the draughts. You see I am well here, with a small fire – but this can be a very draughty house ...

Emma smiles at him.

79b   INTERIOR. DONWELL ABBEY. INNER COURTYARD. *day*

Emma is crossing the courtyard. Frank Churchill comes in, hot and cross.

FRANK: Ah! Miss Woodhouse. Where is everybody? I suppose there was hardly much point in my coming – the party will be breaking up I suppose – I met one as I came. Madness in such weather! Absolute madness!

He is very abstracted – hardly noticing Emma at all.

EMMA: What delayed you?

FRANK: Oh – Mrs Churchill – one of her nervous seizures ... This heat is really too much –

EMMA: You will soon be cooler if you sit still.

FRANK: Yes, thank you – but I must go back again. I could very ill be spared – but such a point was made of my coming!

EMMA: But you will come tomorrow on our outing to Box Hill.

FRANK: No, it will not be worth while. If I come, I shall be cross.

EMMA: Then pray stay at Richmond.

FRANK: But if I do, I shall be crosser still, thinking of you all there without me.

EMMA: These are difficulties you must settle for yourself. Choose your own degree of crossness.

She says this with some asperity, so that Frank takes proper notice of her.

FRANK: You are quite right. I am an absolute bear today. I shall leave you. If I come to Box Hill, I promise to be in good temper. Good day.

He turns on his heel and off he goes. 'Well,' thinks Emma. 'Curiouser and curiouser.'

8 0   EXTERIOR. BOX HILL. *day*

Two carriages, and Mr Weston, Knightley and Frank Churchill on horseback. The Eltons and Jane Fairfax and Miss Bates get down from one carriage, Emma and Harriet from the other.

Servants start lugging the hampers and napery up the hill. Grooms look after the gentlemen's horses. Knightley looks after Jane Fairfax and Miss Bates. Mrs Elton looks up the hill.

MRS ELTON: So this is Box Hill. Well, I am very glad to see it.

They start the climb. The Eltons together, desperate to be first up the hill, then Frank being very gallant with Emma and Harriet, then Knightley with Jane and Miss Bates. Mr Weston trying to be with everybody.

FRANK: [*to Emma*] Let me say at once how much I'm obliged to you for telling me to come today.

That spoken quick, low, and intimate – then turning to Harriet.

FRANK: Miss Woodhouse found me very cross and fatigued yesterday, and almost determined to go away for ever ...

HARRIET: For ever?

FRANK: Well, for a while, and at least as far as Switzerland, but thanks to her, you see, here I am.

HARRIET: [*shyly*] I am very glad she did persuade you.

FRANK: [*warmly*] Thank you, Miss Smith. We passed Dr Perry on our way here – on horseback – what happened to Perry's plan to set up a carriage, Father?

MR WESTON: I heard of no such plan.

FRANK: Yes – you wrote of it in a letter.

MR WESTON: No, not I – I never heard of it.

FRANK: Oh Lord. How strange!

He turns round and looks at Jane and for some reason her expression makes him burst out laughing.

FRANK: Then I suppose – then I suppose I must have dreamt it! Come, Miss Woodhouse! Come, Miss Smith! Best foot forward!

81   EXTERIOR. BOX HILL. *day*

On top of the hill. As the servants lay out the picnic in the background, the idle rich pass the time till lunch. The Eltons stand about irritably. Right in the foreground, Frank tips out alphabet letters from a box on to the white cloth that has been spread. He is very much Emma's playmate – the game is to tease Jane, who is both with them, and not with them, so to speak. As he does it, Harriet comes up eagerly.

HARRIET: Are you going to play anagrams? I am never any good at them.

FRANK: But Miss Fairfax is to be a governess I understand, so she can teach us all ... What do you think this could be, Miss Fairfax?

He puts a jumbled word in front of Jane. She looks at him, picks it up, looks at the letters in her hand, looks back at him and puts them down, still jumbled up.

HARRIET: Oh! May I try? [*Picking up the letters:*] Oh dear ... R ... B ... U ... L ... no, I can't do it at all!

Knightley has come up to watch.

KNIGHTLEY: May I?

HARRIET: Oh, please!

	He rearranges the letters very quickly.
HARRIET:	BLUNDER! Oh, why could I not see it?
	Jane looks distressed. Frank is smiling unabashed. Knightley's keen gaze.
FRANK:	Here's one for you, Miss Woodhouse.
	He hands it to her with a mischievous smile. She does it very quickly, perhaps we could see it, in bright close up in her hand … DIXON!
EMMA:	For shame! Here, take it – I don't want it.
	But she is enjoying the joke as much as he is. Frank's near enough to Emma to whisper:
FRANK:	Shall I give it to her?
EMMA:	No, no, you must not!
FRANK:	Miss Fairfax – would you care to apply yourself to this?
	He gives her the letters. As she looks at them, Knightley is able to see them. He looks back at Frank who stares back at him innocently. And Emma, who looks guilty.
	In on Jane. She looks angry and deeply hurt. She throws the letters down into the pile. She looks at Frank, who smiles back at her.
JANE:	I didn't know …
	[The feeling is she is going to say 'I didn't know you could be so cruel.']
JANE:	… I didn't know that proper names were allowed.
	She gets up and walks away. Harriet's baffled face. Knightley's keen gaze. Emma wilts a bit under it. Frank doesn't.
MR WESTON:	Come, what do you all do there? Are you not hungry?
	The servants have laid out a tremendous spread not far away. As the toffs move over, Knightley contrives a moment with Emma:
KNIGHTLEY:	May I ask what the joke was, Emma, that caused so much entertainment on one side, and so much distress on the other?
EMMA:	Oh – nothing – it was a silly private joke, that's all.

KNIGHTLEY: Was it. Emma – are you sure you understand the degree of acquaintance between those two?

EMMA: Between Frank Churchill and Jane Fairfax? [*laughing*] Could you really think that? There is nothing between them – no attachment at all. That is, I presume there is none on her side – but I know there is nothing on his.

Knightley startled by this. To him, the latter part of Emma's speech implies that there is an attachment, or at least some close relationship, between Emma and Frank Churchill.

82 EXTERIOR. BOX HILL. THE PICNIC. *day*

The toffs lounging round eating and drinking. Down by the coaches the coachmen are having theirs.

On top of Box Hill, a little breeze moves the grass. We can hear bees buzzing. Mrs Elton, fanning herself, looking discontented. Miss Bates chuntering on, in the hearing of both Jane and Knightley. Frank very attentive to Emma, but very alert to Jane's reactions.

MISS BATES: How strange that Mr Frank Churchill should mention Mr Perry's carriage – for it was quite a secret, you know – nobody knew but ourselves – and Jane, of course, and now for Mr Churchill to dream of it – dreams are very extraordinary things I think!

She says it quite innocently. Jane distressed. Knightley alert. Looks over to where Frank is flirting with Emma.

EMMA: You are in much better spirits today.

FRANK: That is because I am under your command.

EMMA: Can't you command yourself?

Round about here, everyone else falls silent – just one of those accidents – only Knightley is really intent on overhearing if he can. Frank, in his wickedly mischievous mood, doesn't care if Jane overhears him. He wants to make her suffer.

FRANK: I don't believe I can. I believe I'm completely under your influence.

EMMA: Since when?

FRANK: Since I saw you first, in February.

EMMA:	[*softly*] I think you should lower your voice. No one else is speaking.
FRANK:	I'm not saying anything to be ashamed of.
	He stands up and proclaims.
FRANK:	I saw you first in February! Let everybody hear it, from Mickleham to Dorking! I saw Miss Emma Woodhouse first in February! There!
	Reverting to a more conversational tone, but addressing everyone:
FRANK:	Now – we are a very dull party, and that will not do. Ladies and gentlemen, I am ordered by Miss Woodhouse to say that she desires to know what you are all thinking.
KNIGHTLEY:	Is Miss Woodhouse sure that she would like to hear what we are all thinking?
EMMA:	Oh, no! Upon no account. It's the very last thing I would stand the brunt of just now.
	[*Jane Austen says she is 'laughing as carelessly as she could'.*]
MRS ELTON:	Ordered by Miss Woodhouse, indeed! I was never in any circle before where I was ordered or required to do anything, or one where young ladies ordered married women to do this or that!
MR ELTON:	I think it is only a kind of joke, Augusta.
MRS ELTON:	Joke indeed. Some people don't seem to understand proper decorum at all.
	She is aiming this at Emma rather than Frank. Frank tries to save the situation.
FRANK:	In that case – Miss Woodhouse orders me to say that she requires something entertaining from each of you! It can be one very clever thing – or two moderately clever things – or three very dull things indeed!
	Mrs Elton to Mr Elton but meant to be heard:
MRS ELTON:	Oh! More of her orders! Intolerable!
	Mrs Elton and Emma almost seem to be squaring up to each other for a good hair-pulling session when Miss Bates good-naturedly comes in with:
MISS BATES:	Well, I am happy to oblige, Miss Woodhouse – three very dull things indeed, that will just do for me, you know. I shall be sure to say three dull things as soon as ever I open my mouth, shan't I? Do not you all think I shall?
	She is looking round feeling she's almost been witty, certainly said the right thing at the right time. Emma can't resist.
EMMA:	Yes, but there may be a difficulty for you Miss Bates. You will be limited as to number – only three at once!
	She says it very merrily, but nobody laughs. See Miss Bates' face fall slowly, as the penny drops. Everybody feels horribly embarrassed. No one can think of anything to say.
MISS BATES:	Ah – well – to be sure. [*turning to Knightley*] Yes, I see what she means – I must try and hold my tongue. I must make myself very disagreeable, or she would not have said such a thing to an old friend.
	Emma very conscious of Knightley's eyes on her. She feels awful, but somehow feels bound to brazen it out. Mr Elton rises, ostentatiously, with a big sneer.

MR ELTON: Shall we walk, Augusta?

She takes his arm and gives Emma a horrible look as they go off.

As soon as they are out of earshot:

FRANK: Happy couple! How well they suit each other. Very lucky, marrying as they did on such a short acquaintance formed in a public place! How many a man has committed himself on a short acquaintance, and regretted it the rest of his life!

JANE: Such things do occur, undoubtedly. But only the weakest characters will allow such an unfortunate acquaintance to be an oppression for ever. Excuse me.

She turns and walks off. She puts a lot of feeling into that – seemed indeed on the verge of tears, but angry as well. Emma is completely baffled. She supposes it must be about being in love with Mr Dixon in some way. And now Frank looks all ruffled again, as he did at Donwell. Knightley is glaring at her. This has been a bit of shambles, this picnic.

83   EXTERIOR. BOX HILL. *day. [later]*

All the toffs coming down the hill to the carriages and horses. Everyone is in a bad mood and nobody is talking. Harriet is ahead of Emma and Frank hands her into the carriage, very flashily. Knightley catches Emma up and draws her aside.

KNIGHTLEY: Emma. [*He lets her turn.*] How could you be so unfeeling to Miss Bates? So insolent in your wit to a woman of her age, and of her situation!

EMMA: I couldn't help myself – she is a good creature, but ridiculous you must allow – I
                   dare say she didn't understand me.

KNIGHTLEY: I assure you she did. She felt your full meaning. She has talked of it since – and
                   with more candour and generosity than she got from you.

                   They walk on for a few steps in silence – he's really angry, but well under control,
                   considering what will hit home hardest. This is different from the Robert Martin anger –
                   this time he's less concerned with the consequences than with Emma herself – he can't bear
                   her to let herself down like this.

KNIGHTLEY: When you were a little girl, it was an honour for you to be noticed by Miss
                   Bates. Now it is the other way round; she is poor, she has sunk from the
                   comforts she was born to – and you chose to humble her, to laugh at her,
                   openly, in company? Her situation should secure your compassion, not your
                   ridicule. It was badly done, Emma, badly done, indeed!

                   In on Emma's face, which is turned away from him. She is crying, but he can't see. She
                   feels utterly mortified. He hands her into the carriage and closes the door. She remembers
                   she's taken no leave of him. She turns to him, her eyes beseeching forgiveness, but he's
                   turned and is striding away, giving her no chance.

                   End of Part Four

84   EXTERIOR. HIGHBURY. *day*

                   Emma comes out of Hartfield and walks resolutely into Highbury. Start Miss Bates'
                   voice-over:

MISS BATES: Ah Miss Woodhouse, how kind you are!

85   INTERIOR. BATES' HOUSE. *day*

                   Miss Bates, Mrs Bates and Emma.

MISS BATES: It is so very good of you! Always so good! Jane is not well – she has a fearful
                   headache – it came upon her at Box Hill and it has got worse since – she asks
                   me to make her apologies to you – she cannot leave her bed – but even so, she
                   has determined to accept the post with Mrs Smallridge – she would write today
                   – and so we are to lose her. But a very good family, Mrs Elton assures us – only
                   four miles from Maple Grove!

EMMA: But this is very sudden ... I suppose she must have been making her mind up all
                   day yesterday.

MISS BATES: Yes, I suppose so – it was before tea that she told me of it – stay, no – it must
                   have been after tea, because John the ostler came to say that Mr Frank Churchill
                   is gone away to Richmond and no knowing when he may be back – that was
                   before tea, and it was after tea that Jane spoke to Mrs Elton.

EMMA:	Perhaps Mrs Churchill is ill again.
MISS BATES:	Yes, perhaps that's it. But it is very good of you to come, Miss Woodhouse. So very good – you are always very good.

86   INTERIOR. HARTFIELD. DRAWING-ROOM. *day*

Emma comes into the room to find Knightley sitting with Mr Woodhouse.

MR WOODHOUSE:	Ah, there you are, my dear.

Knightley rises.

KNIGHTLEY:	I wouldn't leave without seeing you – I am going to London to spend a few days with John and Isabella. Have you anything to send or say, besides the 'love' which no one carries?

His manner is very curt. He's all churned up about Emma and Frank Churchill. Emma thinks he's still angry about Miss Bates, and feels scared and timid, in so far as she can feel that.

EMMA:	No, nothing. Isn't this ... a rather sudden scheme?
KNIGHTLEY:	Yes – rather – I have been thinking of it for some little time.

He seems very abrupt – she is wondering if he hates her now.

MR WOODHOUSE:	Dear Emma has been to call on Mrs and Miss Bates, Mr Knightley. She is always so attentive to them!

Emma looks at Knightley, embarrassed. He looks at her with warm regard. And for some seconds. Emma puzzled – if he's not angry with her still, what is he feeling? She cares more than anything for what he feels about her.

He takes her hand, seems about to raise it to his lips – then he lets it go.

KNIGHTLEY:	I must go.

He goes out quickly. We hear the door close, and the front door.

MR WOODHOUSE:	I do not like it, Emma, when people go away. I know they must do it, sometimes, but I do not like it.
EMMA:	Nor I.

87   EXTERIOR. HIGHBURY OUTSKIRTS. *day*

Emma and Harriet walking into town. Harriet is about to announce a momentous decision.

HARRIET:	I have made up my mind that I shall never marry.
EMMA:	Harriet, what makes you say this? I hope it's not in compliment to Mr Elton?
HARRIET:	Oh, no! There is a person I admire – but he is not someone I could ever ... I owe so much to him – and how could anyone not admire him?
EMMA:	And this dates from ... the service he rendered you?

HARRIET:	Oh, yes! When I saw him coming – how noble he looked – what a change, from perfect misery, to perfect happiness! But I mustn't think of him, must I?
EMMA:	[*encouragingly*] Well, stranger things have ... no.

Remembering her resolution, she stops herself.

EMMA:	Dear Harriet. You mustn't let yourself be influenced – by me, especially. From now on I am determined to lead a better life.

Cut to long shot of the two girls outside the Bates' house. Harriet leaves Emma, as Miss Bates pops her head out of the window.

MISS BATES:	Oh, Miss Woodhouse! What can I say? We have such kind neighbours! But Jane has told me to say that she is still quite unequal to receiving anybody – Oh, Miss Woodhouse, her spirits are quite overcome! She has not left her room for three days!

[NO SCENES 88–92]

93   EXTERIOR. FIELDS. *day*

Jane, walking fast, not looking where she's going, tears streaming down her face. Robert Martin looks up from work to see her pass. She doesn't see him.

94   EXTERIOR. RANDALLS. *dawn*

A horseman gallops up towards Randalls. We hear Frank's voice-over:

FRANK:	[*voice-over*] Sir, madam – it is with the deepest sorrow that I must inform you of the death of my aunt Mrs Churchill. She was carried off by a seizure early on Tuesday morning. I was glad to be with her at the last.

As rider dismounts at door and hands letter to the waiting Mr Weston:

FRANK:	[*voice-over*] As to the future, that seems at present uncertain – I shall visit you again as soon as I can.

95   INTERIOR. EMMA'S BEDROOM. HARTFIELD. *night*

Emma and Harriet preparing for dinner. The two maids are putting the finishing touches to their hair.

EMMA:	Well, I am heartily sorry for almost everything I said and thought about Mrs Churchill!
HARRIET:	Yes, poor lady, very sad – so ill, and everybody vexed with her.
EMMA:	Two interesting questions remain: will she have left Mr Frank Churchill enough money to make him independent; and given that, who will he marry, now he is free to make his own choice? I gather that, the stepfather, is a very easy going man, and quite unlike his wife.
HARRIET:	Yes, who will he marry, now he has his choice?
EMMA:	Harriet. I have reformed. My lips are sealed.

96   EXTERIOR. RANDALLS. *day*

> See Frank Churchill mount his horse and ride off, while Mr Weston hurries on foot in the direction of Hartfield.

97   EXTERIOR. HARTFIELD. GARDEN. *day*

> Emma is just going out when she sees Mr Weston just arrived, and looking uncharacteristically agitated.

MR WESTON: Ah – Miss Woodhouse – can you come to Randalls at any time this morning? Mrs Weston wants to see you – can you come?

EMMA: Of course – this moment, if you please.

> They start going right away.

EMMA: But what is the matter? Is she ill?

MR WESTON: No – no – it is something else. Don't be impatient – it will all come out soon enough. Mrs Weston will break it to you better than I can.

> Emma stops dead.

EMMA: Good God! What? Something has happened to Isabella – to the children?

MR WESTON: No, indeed – it is nothing to do with anybody of the name of Knightley. It is to do with – Come, walk on with me. Mrs Weston will not be easy until she has seen you.

98   INTERIOR. RANDALLS. *day*

> Emma and Mrs Weston.

EMMA: What is it, my dear friend? Tell me at once – it will do you good to speak of your distress, whatever it is.

MRS WESTON: I will tell you, Emma. Frank was here this morning. He came to speak to his father on a subject – to announce an attachment – Emma, he is engaged to Jane Fairfax – he has been secretly engaged to her since October last, when they met at Weymouth – it was he who sent the piano – Emma – he was engaged to Jane Fairfax before he ever came here!

> Emma's startled face. She remembers: Frank gazing at Jane at Randalls; Frank and Jane turning from one another as Emma comes into Miss Bates' lodgings; Jane and Frank dancing together, happily; Jane's distress at Box Hill, when she turns on Frank.

> Emma comes out of it seeing Mrs Weston's face blurry at first:

MRS WESTON: It has hurt me, Emma, very much. It has hurt his father too. Some part of his conduct we cannot excuse.

> His behaviour with Emma, she means. Emma reaches forward and takes her hands. Clear now:

EMMA: Let me relieve you on that score at least. There was a time I confess when I liked him – when I liked him very much – and how it came to cease, I don't know – but you may believe me, I am safe. But his behaviour to her! And towards us all – what hypocrisy, what deceit! Here we have been, the whole winter and spring, fancying ourselves on an equal footing of truth and honour ... and all the time ... Oh Lord – how shall I break it to Harriet?

MRS WESTON: Harriet?

99   EXTERIOR. MRS GODDARD'S SCHOOL. *day*

Small girls and great girls tending their gardens in background. But start right in on Harriet's face, amused and incredulous:

HARRIET: Me? Why should you think it would affect me? You don't think I care about Frank Churchill?

EMMA: But Harriet – didn't you say so yourself? Considering the service he rendered you, it was extremely natural.

HARRIET: No. Oh. You have misunderstood me. I meant a much more precious circumstance. I meant ... Mr Knightley – when he asked me to dance.

EMMA: Good God! Oh, Harriet – if I had known you meant Mr Knightley I should never in a million years have encouraged you.

HARRIET: Why should you not? [*timid, but determined*] You said that more wonderful things have happened ... and – why should it not be so?

Emma is appalled.

EMMA: You believe he returns your affection?

HARRIET: Yes, I must say that I do.

EMMA: Has he said anything directly?

HARRIET: No – but he has talked to me in a very particular way – he seemed to be asking whether my affections were engaged –

EMMA: You are sure he was not thinking of Mr Martin?

HARRIET: Mr Martin! No indeed. I hope I know better now than to care for Mr Martin. I should never have thought of Mr Knightley, you know, if you had not encouraged me.

Harriet's pleased at this thought, and thinks Emma will be too. Emma's face. Oh God, now what have I done?

EMMA: Harriet, I will say this – Mr Knightley is the last person in the world to deceive a woman as to his intentions.

HARRIET: [*in raptures*] Oh, Miss Woodhouse!

100   EXTERIOR. HIGHBURY. *day*

Emma going off up the road, school in background.

EMMA: Oh, God, that I had never met her!

In on her face. Emma remembers: Knightley, at the ball, bending over Harriet – she looks up smiling, and takes his hand; Knightley at the ball, dancing with Harriet; Knightley at

Donwell, talking earnestly with Harriet; Knightley at Box Hill solving the puzzle for Harriet and Harriet looking up into his face smiling. Then she imagines: Knightley in wedding gear looking fondly down at his pretty little bride.

EMMA: No!

101 INTERIOR. HARTFIELD DRAWING-ROOM. *day*

Mr Woodhouse, dozing by the fire, half wakes.

MR WOODHOUSE: Did you say anything, my dear?

EMMA: Nothing, Papa.

He sinks back into slumber. The clock ticks. Rain beats against the window. Emma remembers: Knightley taking baby Emma from her.

KNIGHTLEY: You and I shall never be enemies.

Knightley leading her to the dance floor.

KNIGHTLEY: Brother and sister! No, indeed!

Knightley after Box Hill, handing her into the carriage.

KNIGHTLEY: It was badly done, Emma, badly done indeed!

Emma, in the drawing room, tears on her face, stands up as if trying to shake off these tormenting visions. She looks out of the window. She breathes, her mouth close to the glass:

EMMA: I love him. I have always loved him. Oh, what have I done?

102 EXTERIOR. HARTFIELD. *day*

Rain has eased off, sun has [it is to be hoped] broken through. Emma walking forlornly in the garden on the wet grass. She hears the garden door shut and turns to see Knightley walking across the grass to her. She smiles anxiously – he looks very grim.

EMMA: I did not expect to see you so soon.

KNIGHTLEY: I rode back this morning.

EMMA: You must have had a wet ride.

KNIGHTLEY: Yes.

EMMA: I have some news for you.

KNIGHTLEY: Miss Fairfax and Frank Churchill. I have heard it – I had a letter from Mr Weston and came back directly.

Emma tries for a normal cheerful tone.

EMMA: You were probably less surprised than anyone. You had your suspicions – I wish I had attended to them.

She can't keep it up. She feels so down about everything.

EMMA: [*sadly*] But I seem to have been doomed to blindness.

Impulsively, naturally, he takes her hand and draws her arm within his, and presses it against his heart!

KNIGHTLEY: My dearest Emma, time will heal the wound ... I cannot tell you what I feel – abominable scoundrel! He will soon be gone. They will soon be in Yorkshire. I am sorry for her. She deserves a better fate.

EMMA: You are very kind – but you are mistaken. I have never really been attached to Mr Churchill. I am sorry if I gave that impression – as I am sure I did. I have very little to say for my own conduct. My vanity was flattered, and I allowed his attentions. He never wished to make me fall in love with him. It was a blind to conceal his real situation. He has imposed on me – but he hasn't injured me.

They walk on a pace or two before he bursts out:

KNIGHTLEY: He is a most fortunate man! Everything turns out for his good. He meets a young woman at a watering place – gains her affections – she consents to an engagement. He treats her abominably – she bears it like a saint. His aunt is in the way. His aunt dies. He has used everybody ill, and they are all delighted to forgive him. He is a fortunate man indeed!

EMMA: You speak as if you envied him.

KNIGHTLEY: I do envy him, Emma. In one respect I envy him very much.

Emma turns her face away. She thinks Knightley's about to speak of Harriet.

KNIGHTLEY: You don't wish to know what that is?

She has a little struggle with herself – is she up to hearing that he has fallen for Harriet and he wants her approval? No, she doesn't think she is. She doesn't reply.

KNIGHTLEY: You are determined, I see, to have no curiosity, Emma. I must tell you what you will not ask, though I may wish it unsaid the next moment.

EMMA: [*blurts*] Oh, then, don't speak of it! Take a little time, don't commit yourself!

Then she pauses, for he is asking her for something, and she cannot refuse him.

EMMA: I stopped you ungraciously just then ... Yes, I will hear you – if you wish to tell me you are – contemplating something – yes, you may speak to me, as a friend.

KNIGHTLEY: As a friend! Emma, that, I fear – no. I have gone too far for concealment. Tell me, then – have I no chance of ever succeeding?

[Jane Austen says: 'He stopped in his earnestness to look the question, and the expression of his eyes overpowered her.']

KNIGHTLEY: My dearest Emma – for dearest you will always be – tell me at once. Say 'No' if it is to be said.

Emma can't speak. She thinks she's dreaming.

KNIGHTLEY: I can't make speeches, Emma – if I loved you less, I might be able to talk about it more. But you know what I am. You hear nothing but truth from me. I have blamed you, and lectured you, and you have borne it as no other woman in England would have borne it. Bear with the truth I tell you now. My manners may not have much to recommend them. But you understand me – yes, you understand my feelings – and you will return them if you can.

Emma has had time in that speech to collect herself and to know what to say. Rather shyly, I think:

EMMA:	I can – I do return them. I do love you. I believe I always have – though I never knew it until ... yesterday, I think!
KNIGHTLEY:	Then you do consent?
	In a way, he can hardly believe his luck – he didn't come to propose, he came to console and support and rage on her behalf, to be her friend.
EMMA:	I do. I do. This is so strange.
KNIGHTLEY:	I held you in my arms when you were three weeks old.
EMMA:	Do you like me as well now as you did then?
	She raises her face to his. Let them come together ever so slowly, and as their lips meet, whirl tactfully out of it somewhere up high, to show the dynastic couple in each other's arms, locked together at the centre of the whirling universe, etc.

103   INTERIOR. EMMA'S BEDROOM. *night*

Emma gazing into the mirror in a daze of love, suddenly comes to:

EMMA:	Oh, Lord. Harriet!

104   EXTERIOR. HARTFIELD. *day*

Emma coming out of the house, sees Harriet hurrying towards her:

HARRIET:	Oh! Miss Woodhouse! I was just coming to see you.
EMMA:	I was just on my way to the school.
HARRIET:	Oh, Miss Woodhouse you are going to be so angry with me!
EMMA:	No, no, quite the opposite.
HARRIET:	I must tell you now – you will know soon enough – I am going to be married – to Mr Robert Martin!

Emma gobsmacked as Harriet rushes on:

HARRIET: He came to the school – he was so polite and gentleman-like – and he told me his feelings had never changed – that he loved me still – that he had tried to overcome it but not been able to – and Mr Knightley had encouraged him to try again – he is so good – and I found I couldn't say no – in fact – I believe I have truly been in love with – dear Robert all the time! Oh, dear Miss Woodhouse – say you will forgive me – and think kindly of me – though I understand you will have to give me up and not see me any more.

EMMA: Oh, Harriet! This is – very good news indeed! I – I hope you'll be very happy.

Harriet enraptured:

HARRIET: Oh, Miss Woodhouse!

They embrace, right out there on the road. Not very decorous, but there you go.

105 INTERIOR. HARTFIELD. *night*

Mr Woodhouse fills the screen.

MR WOODHOUSE: What are you thinking of, Emma? No, I do not think this is a good idea at all. Think of poor Isabella. Think of poor Miss Taylor. You had much better not get married. I intend no reflection on Mr Knightley – indeed he is the best of men – but you would both do much better to stay as you are.

EMMA: But I love him, father, and he loves me.

MR WOODHOUSE: Yes, yes, that may very well be, but you had much better not get married. What should I do, if you go from Hartfield? You had much better stay here. Yes. You had much better stay here and not get married. Yes, that would be the best thing.

Now we see Knightley, next to Emma.

KNIGHTLEY: My dear sir, Emma and I have discussed this, and we have agreed that there could be no question of Emma's leaving you. And we understand that you would be much happier here at Hartfield, rather than removing to Donwell Abbey. Therefore ...

EMMA: Mr Knightley has offered to come and live with us here, as long as – as long as you wish it, Papa. Isn't that good of him? He will be here always for you to consult him on business – or to write letters for you – to keep you company – wouldn't you be glad to have him always on the spot?

MR WOODHOUSE: Yes, yes, indeed, very glad – but we see him every day as it is. Why can we not go on as we did before?

EMMA: We see him every day – but we are alone at night! Papa – I have heard that the chicken thieves have returned to the neighbourhood! Not two nights ago, they broke into Mrs Weston's poultry house and stole all her turkeys!

MR WOODHOUSE: Oh!

EMMA: Would you not be happier, knowing that Mr Knightley will be in the house?

Mr Woodhouse thinks about it.

MR WOODHOUSE: Why yes, Emma. I believe I would.

106 EXTERIOR. COUNTRYSIDE. *day*

Donwell Abbey in the background. Knightley looking at his men harvesting ... the hay being hoisted high, natural rhythms, the poetry of work, all that ... Robert Martin goes by along the lane on his haycart, all glowing and brown and gleaming with sweat, all his muscles bulging and his heart full of happiness. The two chaps salute each other.

107 EXTERIOR. DONWELL ABBEY. *evening*

All this is very optimistic, but what we want is one of those golden late summer evenings or the feel of it – harvest home, all that. A lot of people going in, including Robert Martin and his sister and other people of that ilk, as well as Mr and Mrs Elton.

MRS ELTON: Well I declare! Has Knightley invited his tenants?

107a INTERIOR. CORRIDOR AND DONWELL ABBEY. *evening*

The Eltons enter behind the Martins.

MRS ELTON: Are we to sit down with hobbledehoys?

They walk into the great hall where everything is laid out for a great harvest supper. A pig is being roasted on a spit, etc.

MR ELTON: These great men can be eccentric, Augusta my love – and I believe harvest suppers are traditional ...

MRS ELTON: In my opinion eccentricity can go too far – nothing like this was ever seen at Maple Grove!

108 INTERIOR. DONWELL ABBEY. *evening. [later]*

Tables on three sides, Knightley and Emma and Mr Woodhouse and the Westons on the top table, work out the rest later, Harriet is sitting next to Mrs Goddard with Robert Martin and his sister on the other side, she looks very happy. Knightley rises.

KNIGHTLEY: Ladies and gentlemen – friends. We have been blessed this year again with a good harvest. I have been blessed in another way too.

He looks down fondly at Emma and she smiles up at him.

KNIGHTLEY: By next harvest, I shall be living at Hartfield, but I assure you all I shall still be farming my estate, and looking after you all. There will be stability. There will be continuation – though my life is to change. I ask you to drink the health of the lady who has made me the happiest man on Earth: Miss Emma Woodhouse.

Everybody gets up and raises their glasses.

EVERYBODY: Miss Emma Woodhouse!

ONE OF THE
TENANTS: And Mr Knightley!

A nicely ragged but heartfelt chorus of 'Miss Woodhouse and Mr Knightley'. Nice to look through a lot of people at Emma and Knightley sitting together looking like a happy couple.

MRS ELTON: [*to Mr Elton*] Poor Knightley. This is a sad business for him.

109   INTERIOR. DONWELL ABBEY. *night. later*

The informal bit after the meal – people mingling – mostly keeping their social places, but … Emma looks over and sees Harriet with Robert Martin and his sister. She walks over to them – and people see her doing it – Mrs Elton is amazed. Harriet sees her coming, thinks, 'Oh gosh, this is the big moment, will I be up to it':

HARRIET: Miss Woodhouse – may I have the honour of presenting Mr Robert Martin?

He bows.

ROBERT MARTIN: Delighted, ma'am.

EMMA: [*offering her hand*] And so am I. I hope you will both be very happy – and I hope that you will come and visit us at Hartfield very soon, with your sister, of course, and Miss Smith.

Miss Martin curtseys. Harriet's in heaven. Over with the Eltons:

MRS ELTON: Did you see that, Mr E? Wait till I tell them about this at Maple Grove.

MR ELTON: Well, I hope her pride will be contented now …

As he sees Knightley coming up to join Emma, and Emma taking his arm fondly without needing to look at him:

MR ELTON: I suppose she always meant to catch Knightley if she could.

MRS ELTON: And now she's making him go and live at Hartfield!

Mr Woodhouse is in shot, with Miss Bates telling him about Mr Perry or something.

MR ELTON: Rather he than I!

Now John and Isabella come up to Emma – Isabella kissing her.

ISABELLA: [*tearfully*] Oh, Emma – such happiness!

JOHN KNIGHTLEY: Congratulations, Emma.

EMMA: I know you think the good fortune is all on my side!

JOHN KNIGHTLEY: I? Not at all, not at all!

EMMA: You needn't deny it – for this once I agree with you!

Emma catches Jane's eye – they both hesitate – then they decide to risk it. We should contrive a relatively private place for them where they won't be overheard, though Frank is looking at them with lively interest.

EMMA: Miss Fairfax – let me apologize now for any of my conduct that may have hurt you. I can't forgive myself unless you will forgive me.

JANE:	No, indeed – I was unhappy, but I brought it on myself. I always had a part to act – so cold and aritificial – I know I must have disgusted you.
EMMA:	Please – say no more. Shall we forgive each other at once?
JANE:	Thank you. Oh, if you knew how I longed to be open with you!

[Same scene, later:] Emma is looking fondly over at Knightley, who is talking to Jane, as Frank saunters up.

FRANK:	Isn't she lovely? Did you ever see such a skin? Such smoothness.
EMMA:	I have always admired her complexion, though I remember a time when you found fault with her for being so pale.

Frank laughs.

FRANK:	What an impudent dog I am. Can you forgive me, Miss Woodhouse?
EMMA:	If she can forgive you, so can I, I suppose.
FRANK:	She does forgive me. She is a complete angel. Look at her. Observe the turn of her throat. You will be glad to hear that my Uncle Churchill means to give her all my aunt's jewels. Won't they be beautiful against that skin?
EMMA:	Very beautiful.

She may by now be suspecting that she is being drawn into a not altogether pleasant sex game. He moves closer:

FRANK:	How delighted I am to see you again! – and in such excellent looks. I wouldn't have missed this meeting for the world.

Jane can see them, but is not in earshot. Mr Woodhouse becomes audible, talking to Miss Bates.

MR WOODHOUSE:	No, you should not hesitate – you can never send too often for Perry, if you suspect the slightest disorder!
FRANK:	[*raising his voice*] Ah, yes, Perry! My friend Mr Perry! Yes, how does he travel now? Has he set up his carriage?

He watches her, bright-eyed, demonic.

FRANK:	Such an extraordinary dream of mine! She hears us, she hears us – I see it in her cheek! Ah, she blushes! She pretends to listen to the others, but she can attend to nothing else!

He moves towards her, confident in his mastery, confident that he can treat her any way he likes.

JANE:	How you can bear such recollections is extraordinary to me. They will sometimes obtrude – but how you can court them!

He laughs, but it is not a funny situation. Emma looks at him, looks at them, and sees what their marriage will be. He will flirt with other women, he will probably make love to a lot of other women, he will parade it, he will confess, he will expect to be forgiven, he will make her life a misery.

Knightley comes over to Emma and offers his hand.

KNIGHTLEY:	Will you dance with me, Emma?

As she takes his hand, gracefully and joyfully, he teases:

KNIGHTLEY: You and I are not so much brother and sister as to make it improper, you know.

EMMA: [laughing] Brother and sister! No, indeed.

The room parts as Knightley leads Emma to the top of the room. Frank and Jane then Harriet and Robert follow.

The rest fall in behind, all in their places. The band strikes up and the three betrothed couples dance the first figure, before everyone joins in.

110   EXTERIOR.   DONWELL ABBEY. night

Across the lawn, we see the lighted windows and hear the music faintly.

Crash! The chicken thieves have burst the padlock. Much squawking of chickens. And now we see feathers and loose hens all over the lawn. The cock struts out.

COCK: Cock-a-doodle-doo!

Fade out

The cast and crew

CAST CREDITS

Emma Woodhouse	**Kate Beckinsale**	*Dancers*	**Roy Ashby**
Mr Woodhouse	**Bernard Hepton**		**Rebecca Elliott**
Knightley	**Mark Strong**		**Nick French**
Mrs Weston	**Samantha Bond**		**Michael Haighton**
Mr Weston	**James Hazeldine**		**Juliet James**
Harriet Smith	**Samantha Morton**		**Mark Andrew Joslin**
Mr Elton	**Dominic Rowan**		**Bryan Payne**
Mrs Elton	**Lucy Robinson**		**Elizabeth Renihan**
Miss Bates	**Prunella Scales**		**Donna Ross**
Mrs Bates	**Sylvia Barter**		**Stephen Russell**
Frank Churchill	**Raymond Coulthard**		**Stephen Speed**
Jane Fairfax	**Olivia Williams**		**Dee-Dee Wilde**
John Knightley	**Guy Henry**		**Wendy Woodbridge**
Isabella Knightley	**Dido Miles**		
Mr Perry	**Peter Howell**		
Mrs Goddard	**Judith Coke**		
Robert Martin	**Alistair Petrie**		
Elizabeth Martin	**Phoebe Welles-Cooper**		
Miss Otway	**Tabby Harris**		
Thomas (the butler)	**Neville Phillips**		
Henry Knightley	**Sunny Jim Dickson**		

CREW CREDITS

Produced by	**Sue Birtwistle**	*Property Master*	**Danny Euston**
Directed by	**Diarmuid Lawrence**	*Dressing Props*	**Dempsey Cook**
Screenplay	**Andrew Davies**		**Ray Morgan**
Music	**Dominic Muldowney**	*Standby Props*	**Ian Newton**
Director of Photography	**Remi Adefarasin**		**Clive Brown**
Production Designer	**Don Taylor**	*Construction Manager*	**Roger Wilkins**
Costume Designer	**Jenny Beavan**	*Construction Carpenter*	**Frank Saunders**
Make-up Designer	**Mary Hillman**	*Standby Carpenter*	**Paul Duff**
Film Editor	**Don Fairservice**	*Construction Painter*	**Mark Roberts**
Sound Recordist	**Jim Greenhorn**	*Standby Painter*	**Tom Roberts**
Casting Director	**Janey Fothergill**	*Carpenter*	**Gareth Wilkins**
Script Editor	**Susie Conklin**	*Painter*	**Peter Hasledene**
Choreographer	**Jane Gibson**	*Painter*	**Steve Roberts**
Location Manager	**Sue Quinn**	*Standby Rigger*	**Greg Press**
Location Assistant	**Joseph Jayawardena**	*Storeman*	**David Dibden**
Art Director	**Jo Graysmark**	*Food Stylist*	**Debbie Brodie**
Assistant Art Director	**Frances Bennett**	*Food Assistant*	**Katherine Tidy**
Set Decorator	**John Bush**	*Horsemaster*	**Debbie Kaye**
Buying Assistant	**Anita Goundar**	*Special Effects*	**Peter Hutchinson & Co.**

Stunt Co-ordinator	**Andreas Petrides**	*Dialogue Coach*	**Joan Washington**
Stunt Performers	**Lyndon Hellewell**	*Voice Coach*	**Patsy Rodenburg**
	Guy List	*Dubbing Editor*	**Andy Kennedy**
Wardrobe Supervisor	**Anna Kot**	*Assitant Film Editor*	**Bridgette Corbett**
Costume Assistant	**Stephen Miles**	*Production Accountant*	**Susan Nicholson**
Costume Assistant	**Carla Pope**	*Assistant Accountant*	**Stephen Naulls**
Make-up Artist	**Patricia Kirkman**	*Casting Assistant*	**Elaine Vergette**
Make-up Artist	**Penny Bell**	*Production Co-ordinator*	**Pat Bryan**
Script Supervisor	**Sue Clegg**	*Production Secretary*	**Deborah Armstrong**
First Assistant Director	**Edward Brett**	*Production Runner*	**Jonathan Rippon**
Second Assistant Director	**Dominic Fysh**	*Floor Runner*	**Paul Sykes**
Third Assistant Director	**Connie Boylan**		**Daniel Antony John**
Camera Operator	**Sean Savage**	*Rushes Runner*	**Aden Turner**
Focus Puller	**Ben Wilson**	*Post-Production Supervisor*	**Tina Hetherington**
Clapper Loader	**Sarah Bartles-Smith**		
Grip	**John Arnold**	*Executive in charge of Production for Meridian*	
Sound Maintenance	**Simon Firsht**		**Philip Leach**
Gaffer	**Jimmy Wilson**	*Associate Producer*	**Joy Spink**
Best Boy	**Barrie More**	*Executive Producer for A&E*	**Delia Fine**
Electrician	**Tony Burns**	*Executive Producer for Meridian*	**Simon Lewis**
Generator Operator	**Mitch Spooner**		
Assistant Choreographer	**Jack Murphy**		

A UNITED FILM & TELEVISION production
for MERIDIAN BROADCASTING
in association with CHESTERMEAD LTD and
A&E NETWORK ©1996

MERIDIAN

Locations

Hartfield
Trafalgar Park
Downton
Near Salisbury
Wiltshire

Highbury Village
Lacock Village
Near Chippenham
Wiltshire

Randalls
Dorney Court
Windsor
Berkshire

Donwell Abbey
Broughton Castle
Broughton
Near Banbury

Sudley Castle
Near Winchcombe
Gloucestershire

Stanway House
Near Broadway
Gloucestershire

**Abbey Mill Farm,
Donwell Strawberry Beds, Derelict Cottages,
the Sea off Weymouth**
Thame Park
Near Thame
Oxfordshire

'This one half hour had given to each the same precious certainty of being beloved' (Jane Austen).

SUE BIRTWISTLE started work as an actress with the Belgrade Theatre in Education Company Coventry, before becoming Director of the Royal Lyceum Theatre in Education Company in Edinburgh. She was the founder director of the Nottingham Playhouse Roundabout Company. She served as a member of the Arts Council Drama Panel and toured many plays in Europe. She has written two plays for children. Her television credits as producer include the award-winning *Hotel du Lac* and Tony Harrison's 'v'. She has also produced *Scoop*, *Dutch Girls*, *Or Shall We Die?*, *Educating Marmalade* (BAFTA nomination), *Ball-Trap on the Côte Sauvage*, *Oi for England* and the highly acclaimed *Pride and Prejudice*. Sue Birtwistle lives in London with her husband, Richard Eyre, and has one daughter.

SUSIE CONKLIN grew up in the American south-west and studied English literature at Columbia University and Scottish and Irish literature at Aberdeen University. She joined BBC Television as a production trainee in 1990, and worked on a variety of arts, education and documentary programmes before joining the drama department. There she worked as the script-editor on the award-winning productions of *Middlemarch*, *Between the Lines* and *Pride and Prejudice*. In 1995 she joined Granada Television's drama department, where her credits as script editor include the second series of *Band of Gold*, and adaptations of Daniel Defoe's *Moll Flanders* and Robert Louis Stevenson's *The Ebb Tide*. Susie lives in Buckinghamshire with her husband.

The Making of Pride and Prejudice is also available in Penguin.

ACKNOWLEDGEMENTS

The authors would like to thank:

The cast and crew of *Emma* for their interest, photographs and anecdotes;

The following for submitting to trial by interview:
Andrew Davies, Diarmuid Lawrence, Kate Beckinsale, Mark Strong, Don Taylor, Jenny Beavan, Mary Hillman, Remi Adefarasin, Jane Gibson, Janey Fothergill, Sue Quinn, John Bush, Debbie Brodie, Stephen Miles, Patricia Kirkman and the Lady Seye and Sele;

Barry Ledingham for his invaluable help with the photographs;
Maya Maraj for her support and encouragement;
Clare Brown for all her hard work;
Julie Martin for designing the book;
and Pat Silburn for being the US Cavalry on a difficult Bank Holiday weekend.

PHOTOGRAPHS IN THE BOOK BY:

Remi Adefarasin	Matthew Ford	Sue Quinn
Michael Birt	Neal Genower	Bill Robinson
Sue Birtwistle	Val Goulden	Tony Russell
John Bush	Jo Graysmark	Geoff Shields
Ivan Coleman	Patricia Kirkman	Peter Simpkin
Paul Duff	Fatima Namdar	Don Taylor

[No photograph to be reproduced without permission.]

Screenplay reproduced with kind permission of Meridian Broadcasting Limited. Copyright 1996

Autumn woodcut by Val Biro from 'British Folk Customs' by Christina Hole.